Celebrity Culture

Other Books of Related Interest:

Opposing Viewpoints Series

American Values

Corporate Social Responsibility

Ethics

Mass Media

At Issue Series

Are Athletes Good Role Models?

Beauty Pageants

Reality TV

The Wealth Divide

Current Controversies Series

Internet Activism

Media Ethics

Rap and Hip Hop

"Congress shall make no law . . . abridging the freedom of speech, or of the press."

First Amendment to the US Constitution

The basic foundation of our democracy is the First Amendment guarantee of freedom of expression. The Opposing Viewpoints series is dedicated to the concept of this basic freedom and the idea that it is more important to practice it than to enshrine it.

OPPOSING VIEWPOINTS® SERIES

Celebrity Culture

Noah Berlatsky, Book Editor

GREENHAVEN PRESS
A part of Gale, Cengage Learning

GALE
CENGAGE Learning·

Farmington Hills, Mich • San Francisco • New York • Waterville, Maine
Meriden, Conn • Mason, Ohio • Chicago

Patricia Coryell, *Vice President & Publisher, New Products & GVRL*
Douglas Dentino, *Manager, New Products*
Judy Galens, *Acquisitions Editor*

For more information, contact:
Greenhaven Press
27500 Drake Rd.
Farmington Hills, MI 48331-3535
Or you can visit our Internet site at gale.cengage.com

For product information and technology assistance, contact us at

Gale Customer Support, 1-800-877-4253
For permission to use material from this text or product, submit all requests online at www.cengage.com/permissions

Further permissions questions can be emailed to permissionrequest@cengage.com

Articles in Greenhaven Press anthologies are often edited for length to meet page require-ments. In addition, original titles of these works are changed to clearly present the main thesis and to explicitly indicate the author's opinion. Every effort is made to ensure that Greenhaven Press accurately reflects the original intent of the authors. Every effort has been made to trace the owners of copyrighted material.

Cover image © Yuganov Konstantin/Shutterstock.com.

LIBRARY OF CONGRESS CATALOGING-IN-PUBLICATION DATA

Celebrity culture / edited by Noah Berlatsky.
        pages cm -- (Opposing viewpoints) Summary: "Opposing Viewpoints is the leading source for libraries and classrooms in need of current-issue materials. The viewpoints are selected from a wide range of highly respected sources and publications"-- Provided by publisher.
        Includes bibliographical references and index.
        ISBN 978-0-7377-7246-3 (hardback) -- ISBN 978-0-7377-7247-0 (paperback)
        1. Celebrities--Juvenile literature. 2. Popular culture--Juvenile literature. I. Ber-latsky, Noah, editor.
        HM621.C45 2015
        306--dc23
                                                                    2014042254

Printed in the United States of America
1 2 3 4 5 6 7 19 18 17 16 15

Contents

Chapter 3: How Does Celebrity Culture Affect Particular Groups?

Chapter 4: Is Celebrity Culture Changing?

Why Consider Opposing Viewpoints?

> *"The only way in which a human being can make some approach to knowing the whole of a subject is by hearing what can be said about it by persons of every variety of opinion and studying all modes in which it can be looked at by every character of mind. No wise man ever acquired his wisdom in any mode but this."*
>
> *John Stuart Mill*

In our media-intensive culture it is not difficult to find differing opinions. Thousands of newspapers and magazines and dozens of radio and television talk shows resound with differing points of view. The difficulty lies in deciding which opinion to agree with and which "experts" seem the most credible. The more inundated we become with differing opinions and claims, the more essential it is to hone critical reading and thinking skills to evaluate these ideas. Opposing Viewpoints books address this problem directly by presenting stimulating debates that can be used to enhance and teach these skills. The varied opinions contained in each book examine many different aspects of a single issue. While examining these conveniently edited opposing views, readers can develop critical thinking skills such as the ability to compare and contrast authors' credibility, facts, argumentation styles, use of persuasive techniques, and other stylistic tools. In short, the Opposing Viewpoints Series is an ideal way to attain the higher-level thinking and reading skills so essential in a culture of diverse and contradictory opinions.

In addition to providing a tool for critical thinking, Opposing Viewpoints books challenge readers to question their own strongly held opinions and assumptions. Most people form their opinions on the basis of upbringing, peer pressure, and personal, cultural, or professional bias. By reading carefully balanced opposing views, readers must directly confront new ideas as well as the opinions of those with whom they disagree. This is not to argue simplistically that everyone who reads opposing views will—or should—change his or her opinion. Instead, the series enhances readers' understanding of their own views by encouraging confrontation with opposing ideas. Careful examination of others' views can lead to the readers' understanding of the logical inconsistencies in their own opinions, perspective on why they hold an opinion, and the consideration of the possibility that their opinion requires further evaluation.

Evaluating Other Opinions

To ensure that this type of examination occurs, Opposing Viewpoints books present all types of opinions. Prominent spokespeople on different sides of each issue as well as well-known professionals from many disciplines challenge the reader. An additional goal of the series is to provide a forum for other, less known, or even unpopular viewpoints. The opinion of an ordinary person who has had to make the decision to cut off life support from a terminally ill relative, for example, may be just as valuable and provide just as much insight as a medical ethicist's professional opinion. The editors have two additional purposes in including these less known views. One, the editors encourage readers to respect others' opinions—even when not enhanced by professional credibility. It is only by reading or listening to and objectively evaluating others' ideas that one can determine whether they are worthy of consideration. Two, the inclusion of such viewpoints encourages the important critical thinking skill of objectively evaluating an author's credentials and bias. This evaluation will illuminate an author's reasons for taking a particular stance on an issue and will aid in readers' evaluation of the author's ideas.

It is our hope that these books will give readers a deeper understanding of the issues debated and an appreciation of the complexity of even seemingly simple issues when good and honest people disagree. This awareness is particularly important in a democratic society such as ours in which people enter into public debate to determine the common good. Those with whom one disagrees should not be regarded as enemies but rather as people whose views deserve careful examination and may shed light on one's own.

Thomas Jefferson once said that "difference of opinion leads to inquiry, and inquiry to truth." Jefferson, a broadly educated man, argued that "if a nation expects to be ignorant and free . . . it expects what never was and never will be." As individuals and as a nation, it is imperative that we consider the opinions of others and examine them with skill and discernment. The Opposing Viewpoints series is intended to help readers achieve this goal.

David L. Bender and Bruno Leone,
Founders

Introduction

"Nearly all well-known cosplayers have been involved in the hobby for years—some close to a decade or more—before gaining widespread notoriety. They bleed cosplay; many of them quite literally, having accidentally stabbed, burnt, and bruised themselves during the costume creation process. And all of them are lifetime geeks!"

—*Brittany Johnston,*
"Examining the Cosplay Celebrity,"
Comicsandcosplay.com,
March 25, 2013

Film stars and music stars are national and even international celebrities, widely discussed and promoted through mainstream media outlets. However, the Internet and social media have made it possible for people to communicate with each other and discuss interests without relying on magazines, newspapers, or television shows. As a result, many communities have begun to have micro-celebrities—individuals who may have thousands, or even millions, of fans, even though they are not followed or promoted by traditional media.

Cosplayers are one such group of micro-celebrities. Cosplay refers to the act of designing and wearing costumes, usually based on fictional characters. Cosplayers often dress up as characters from video games, or from comics or cartoons, especially Japanese manga and anime. Cosplay is very popular at comics, science fiction, and video game conventions. Many fans make their own costumes and dress up. Some of these fans have become famous for their costumes—they are no longer just fans, but celebrities themselves.

Cosplay celebrity often comes with financial opportunities. Comics conventions and related events generate $600 million in ticket sales every year, according to Colin Bertram in an article for NBC Bay Area. Cosplay is a major part of the attraction; online ticketing service Eventbrite found in a survey that 23 percent of men and 50 percent of women put cosplay as one of their top three reasons for attending comics conventions. Celebrity cosplayers can, therefore, be a major attraction at these events, attracting event goers in the same way that a star of *Doctor Who* or an actor in a sci-fi film might.

For instance, one of the biggest international cosplay celebrities is Jessica Nigri. In a June 4, 2014, profile of Nigri at Azcentral.com, Kaila White reports that the cosplay star attends about twenty conventions a year. Nigri's costumes can each cost up to $500 for materials and can take up to fifty hours to make. In return for that effort, though, Nigri has received international fame and lucrative opportunities. She pioneered the practice of making cosplay posters of herself in costume; now orders come in from around the world. In 2012 she got her first offer to be paid to cosplay—$10,000 for ten appearances as the star of the video game *Lollipop Chainsaw*. At age twenty-four, Nigri is working full time as a cosplayer and investing in stocks for the future. According to White's article, Nigri said, "I'm front-end loading because I know everything is going to go south eventually, of course, you know, literally."

As Nigri suggests, and as is common with female celebrities in music or acting, physical appearance is an important aspect of cosplay celebrity. This has drawn some criticism from cosplay fans, who believe cosplay should be more about the costumes and passion for games or cartoons than about physical attractiveness. In an August 29, 2013, post titled "The Problem with Cosplay Celebrity" at the *Bitter Gertrude* blog, the author writes,

As someone who has always been a nerd, usually in the process of varying degrees of hiding my nerdiness, the cosplay scene was like a dream come true. I'd never been involved in a more openly nerdy, less judgmental activity. It was a way to express your enjoyment of a certain thing and enjoy it along with others. The accuracy, complexity, or creativity of the costume was paramount. I remember examining the craftsmanship on one woman's costume as she proudly told me she learned metal working in order to create it.

However, the blogger says, "Cosplay is now dominated by models and women striving to look like models, who sell seductive pictures of themselves posing in sexy costumes." She adds that she does not blame the cosplayers; instead, she says, the problem is the logic of celebrity and traditional beauty standards. "Where once upon a time a cosplayer could be anyone with a costume and a lanyard, the rise of cosplay celebrity has brought with it our culture's oppressive normativity for female (and often male) bodies in display-related activities, and that extends to body size, body type, gender identity, age, and race." She argues that as cosplay has become big business, and as cosplayers have begun to act and look, as well as to be treated, like celebrities, the community has lost some of what she feels made it a welcome alternative to mainstream expectations and standards.

Opposing Viewpoints: Celebrity Culture examines other controversies and discussions surrounding celebrity in chapters titled "Is Celebrity Culture Harmful?," "Is Celebrity Activism Beneficial?," "How Does Celebrity Culture Affect Particular Groups?," and "Is Celebrity Culture Changing?" Many of the issues raised by celebrity cosplayers—the rise of social media, celebrity endorsements, and celebrity reflection of body image—are mirrored in the following chapters on mainstream celebrities and their place in culture and society.

OPPOSING
VIEWPOINTS®
SERIES

CHAPTER 1

Is Celebrity Culture Harmful?

Chapter Preface

O ne of the most controversial changes in celebrity in recent years has been reality television. Reality TV is a genre that generally puts regular people in unusual situations and then films the results; the shows often feature a great deal of interpersonal drama and conflict. Popular reality television shows can catapult unknown, non-celebrities into widespread notoriety.

Reality television shows are popular with networks in part because they are relatively cheap to produce. However, Carlo Strenger argues in a February 23, 2011, article at a *Psychology Today* blog that the genre is loved by viewers precisely because of the way it seems to make celebrity available to everyone. Strenger says,

> Reality TV focuses on the process of transformation that turns an ordinary mortal into a demigod. This process is normally hidden from the spectator's eye. We are not privy to the process that has turned [actors] Brad Pitt and Angelina Jolie, George Clooney and Scarlett Johansson into celebrities. We only see the end result of the human already transformed into a demigod. But our culture is obsessed with this transformation; we want to see the miracle happen.

Many commentators have been very critical of the popularity of reality TV shows. Daniel Dominguez in a 2012 article at the Smosh website, for example, attacks the genre for pushing higher quality drama and informational television programs off the air. He also argues that the shows are deceptive because they "do not portray 'reality.' They portray a reality that is somehow both vastly more active, and yet infinitely more dull than our own." Finally, he says reality TV shows are in the business of "enabling the wretched." Before reality TV, he says, "when someone was having personal problems, people would help them. Okay, maybe I'm giving us too much credit, but we at least wouldn't shove a camera in their face." Reality TV shows, he suggests, encourage the consumption of other people's misery.

On the other hand, Sadie Gennis in a June 27, 2013, post at *TV Guide* argues that reality TV programs can be good for viewers. Gennis says she has learned about home improvements from reality shows and that *Newlyweds: The First Year* has helped her have more realistic expectations for marriage. She also says that reality TV has taught her about other cultures. "Do I think *Shahs'* [*Shahs of Sunset*] Reza and his friends represent all Persians in LA? Of course not, but it's still an in-depth glimpse at part of the world I otherwise never would have known about." She concludes that, "There's nothing wrong with pure entertainment." She notes that dramas on television are often emotionally intense and depressing, whereas reality TV is pure escapism. "For an hour a day, people should be able to escape into the feel-good world of celebrity diving, drunk guidos and silly murder mysteries. Just embrace it and have fun. That's what TV's for, isn't it?"

The following chapter examines other arguments that consider whether celebrity culture is harmful, focusing on issues such as whether celebrity has replaced heroism and the relationship between celebrity and unhealthy body image.

> *"Sharing facts and gossip brings groups together and helps them bond. . . . It's part of the normal functioning of society."*

Celebrity Culture Is Natural and Can Be Beneficial

David Cox

David Cox is a writer and television producer who has contributed to the New Statesman, Prospect, *the* Times, *and numerous other publications. In the following viewpoint, he says that celebrity culture and the enthusiastic or obsessive interest in celebrity lives are often denigrated. However, he points to Stephen Hawking, an astrophysicist who has embraced his own celebrity, as a sign that interest in celebrity culture does not necessarily equate with unintelligence. He also argues that studies show that interest in celebrities bonds people together and leads to greater social engagement. He concludes that interest in celebrity is natural and in many ways beneficial.*

As you read, consider the following questions:

1. According to Cox, the documentary *Hawking* doesn't spend much time explaining Hawking's discoveries. What does he say it focuses on instead?

2. Why did the Greek philosopher Plato disapprove of competition for praise, according to the viewpoint?

3. What benefits does Chris Rojek say that people receive from following celebrities?

Our celebrity culture rarely goes long unbemoaned: earlier this summer [in 2013], Sofia Coppola's [film] *The Bling Ring* prompted another round of hand-wringing. According to the disgruntled, it was absurd that the likes of [socialite and celebrity] Paris Hilton should be famous. It was even more absurd that people should steal celebrities' knickers, and in doing so achieve notoriety of their own. Making a film about the ninnies involved was still more lamentable, and going to see it was almost as bad.

Celebrity Obsession Is Everywhere

All the same, even those most aghast seemed unsurprised: No one can deny that obsession with stardom is rampant. Research has suggested that around 40% of adults expect to enjoy their 15 minutes of fame in some guise or other. Many more are enthralled by those who achieve this goal, often immoderately.

Psychologists at the University of Leicester found that 36% of a sample of 600 adults were afflicted to some degree by what was termed "celebrity-worship syndrome". The most extreme sufferers believed that the object of their ardour knew them, and declared themselves ready to die for their hero.

Thus, celebrity culture has been branded the defining disease of our age, ravaging what remains of our civilisation. New media are seen as rendering the plague terminal, as we spend ever more of our lives reading [comedian] Stephen Fry's tweets and perusing cellulite on the *Mail Online*'s "sidebar of shame".

If only people could attend instead to something that really mattered: They'd soon forget their foolish fondness for fame. Something, perhaps, like the workings of the universe?

[Physicist] Stephen Hawking has actually spent most of his life addressing the conundrums of the cosmos. A forthcoming documentary, *Hawking*, enables him to tell his story in his own words. It reveals that the great man has indeed relished probing the limits of knowledge; but what really seems to excite him is the applause he has elicited from the rabble.

Neither the film nor its protagonist seem anxious to waste much time on explaining the hero's discoveries. Instead, as Hawking turns his life into an imposingly epic narrative, we see him drinking in the adulation in thronged lecture halls, and pursuing bizarre opportunities to bathe in the limelight. We watch him playing along with imbecile chat-show hosts and inflicting on their audiences grotesque attempts at jokey banter. The impression left is that it's fun to prove that nothing existed before the big bang; however, making *The Guinness Book of Records* for authoring the world's longest enduring best seller is yet more gratifying.

Hawking even suggests that his embrace of his then newfound fame caused the breakup of his first marriage. In the film, his first wife, Jane, says he became "the public wunderkind". The couple "were engulfed and then swept away by a wave of fame and fortune. It got rather too much for me to cope with."

The professor deserves points for owning up to his foible, but his scope for denial was perhaps limited. After all, Hawking has played himself on *Star Trek*. He has rescued Lisa Simpson from peril in Springfield [on the *Simpsons*], and threatened to steal Homer's theory that the universe is doughnut-shaped. He has starred with [comedian] Jim Carrey in a TV skit, guested on sitcom *The Big Bang Theory* and appeared regularly on a short-lived show called *TV Offal*. In *Futurama* he voiced his own head in a jar.

Pursuing Fame Is Not New

Less candid telly-dons claim they seek mass exposure only to enlighten the benighted; however, their jealous common-room peers rarely seem convinced. So the love of fame cannot be dismissed as the sole preserve of the witless. Nor is it a fever of our era alone, still less a product of new modes of communication.

Even in the middle ages, Thomas Becket [the murdered Archbishop of Canterbury] could become an idol across Europe without the benefit of social media: Mere word of mouth was enough to generate a vast pilgrimage industry. Technology did indeed expand the ambit of fame, but printing, engraving, photography and the mass media of the 19th and 20th centuries played a bigger role than our own digital gadgetry.

Disapproval of celebrity is no novelty either. By 1637, when [poet John] Milton called fame "that last infirmity of noble mind", the same sentiment had already been voiced by [Roman historian] Tacitus, [Christian theologian] St Augustine and [French essayist Michel de] Montaigne.

Nowadays, even the movies are prepared to join the chorus of disparagement, in spite of the sustenance they derive from celebrity. *The Bling Ring*'s attitude to its subject matter may have been equivocal, but documentaries such as *Starsuckers* and *Videocracy* have been harshly censorious, while qualms have pervaded more illustrious titles ranging from *Sunset Boulevard*, *La Dolce Vita* and *The King of Comedy* to *Bye Bye Birdie*, *To Die For* and *Being John Malkovich*.

Cinema's stars, too, sometimes affect disdain for their own lofty status. Press intrusion, they imply, is awful; promoting their films is a burden. Nonetheless, most of them eagerly grasp the trappings of fame, from money to power, sex and the best restaurant tables. There may be the occasional reclusive Greta Garbo; but there seem to be many more like Katharine Hepburn, who once remarked: "I didn't have any desire to be an actress or to learn how to act. I just wanted to be famous."

Just what is supposed to be wrong with the pursuit of fame is not always made clear. [Greek philosopher] Plato disapproved of competition for praise on the grounds that it would tempt the great to bend to the will of the crowd. It is hard to argue with that, and social degradation remains a fear. Says the novelist Will Self: "A culture that privileges notoriety above other human attributes—talent, power, beauty, et al.—is one in which expertise of any sort has been replaced by a perverse cult of the amateur."

Some seem to believe it is vital for human beings to create their own essence: Depending on others' approval will only lead to disaster. "Fame enslaves the gods and men," according to [Greek philosopher] Heraclitus, and contemporary studies have found that subjects motivated by praise and recognition experience lower well-being than those pursuing internally derived goals.

Those who actually achieve fame are supposedly vulnerable to conditions like "acquired situational narcissism". New York psychiatrist Robert B Millman says this affliction can cause a celebrity to get "so used to everyone looking at him that he stops looking back at them". This may lead to grandiose fantasies, rage and loss of empathy, which can in turn prompt relationship breakdown, addiction and loss of touch with reality.

The Dangers of Fandom

Fandom is held to be hardly less perilous. A Chinese study found that subjects who idolised celebrities performed less well at work or college and enjoyed lower self-esteem than those who looked up to teachers or relations. Other studies have found higher levels of depression, anxiety, stress and general illness, accompanied by increased rates of addiction and crime.

In view of all this, you might wonder why either stars or fans bother; yet there is an answer. The human condition presents everyone, even intellectual giants such as Hawking, with some harrowing realities. For both the famous and their followers, the celebrity culture can make bearable what otherwise would not be.

Death is the most obvious of these existential predicaments. For the ancients, circumventing it was the main point of fame. "Short is my date, but deathless my renown," as [Greek poet] Homer put it. Today, traces of this attitude persist: "Fame! I'm gonna live forever" is the punchline of *Fame*, the musical. Hawking has certainly been forced to confront his own mortality: The documentary reveals that in 1985 his life-support machine would have been turned off during an illness, but for his first wife's intervention. However, death is no longer our only source of unease.

[German philosopher Immanuel] Kant's characterisation of the individual as a speck of sand in an infinity of time has been amply confirmed, in part by Hawking's own work. For us, steeped as we are in self-love and entitlement, insignificance seems to have become insufferable. Today, for many, to be a nonentity is to be a nonentity.

Fame may not eliminate the bleakness of an uncaring cosmos, but it can mitigate its impact. Becoming an acolyte of the elect also seems to help: Devotion earns you a share of your hero's aura. Better surely to find succour in this way than to turn instead to terrorism, serial murder or Internet trolling.

Escaping Loneliness

We also seem desperate to relieve the loneliness of Hawking's universe. Personal relationships are difficult, yet stars whose

"I hate it when you look at celebrity photos in those magazines, you become so catty."

© Richard Jolley, "I hate it when you look at celebrity photos in those magazines, you become so catty," Cartoonstock.com.

narcissism dooms their marriages can bask in the unconditional adulation of their following; the latter in turn enjoy "parasocial interaction" with gorgeous pseudo-chums without fear of rejection or betrayal.

Today, many of us know more about the lives of stars than about those of our relations or friends. The extended family may have withered and community life may have waned; yet we can share the successes and reverses of the famous, and hear them talk back to us on Twitter. If we want to, we can revel in their misfortunes and laugh at them behind their backs, in a way that real-life intimacy does not permit. At sites such as The Ghoul Pool, we can even bet on when they will die.

Such behaviour is condemned as detrimental, but research has shown that keeping up with celebrity news helps teenagers become more independent from their parents and makes them more popular. Psychologist John Maltby of Leicester University, who specialises in social influences on individuals, believes young people can benefit from becoming fans of the same stars. "Sharing facts and gossip brings groups together and helps them bond," he says. "It's part of the normal functioning of society."

Chris Rojek, the professor of sociology at City University [London] and the author of *Fame Attack*, thinks it is not only the young who gain. "Celebrities are informal life coaches. By watching them, people learn how to groom, learn how to wear their hair, learn what to say, learn what opinions are sexy, learn what's right-on and not right-on. They're assimilating all sorts of life-skills." Since such education is widely shared, it can function as a "social adhesive".

Celebrity as Religion

Perhaps, as some suggest, celebrity is becoming our religion. It has its rituals, like red carpet appearances, its relics, like David Beckham T-shirts, and its festivals, like fan conventions. High priests such as [film star] James Dean, [revolutionary fighter] Che Guevara, [singer] Bob Marley and [film star] Marilyn Monroe are canonised after death. Yet if we need some kind of religion to lend transcendence to our lives, we could choose worse than this one, which generates less guilt, cant or strife than most of the more conventional alternatives.

In this communion, the likes of Paris Hilton are not the only kind of pastor. "Nelson Mandela is a celebrity," points out Rojek, "and his influence is pretty positive." Claire Fox, the director of the Institute of Ideas, has her doubts about the celebrity culture, but says: "It's certainly reasonable that someone like Hawking should become a celebrity, because of his important contribution to society."

Quasi-religious icons can use their divinity to worthy effect. Rojek believes that "celebrity advocacy" can be beneficial, even as practised by controversial figures such as Angelina Jolie: "She publicises very effectively the issues in developing countries," he suggests. An American study found that 80% of its sample had discussed the political views of celebrities with friends.

James Bennett, who is Reader in Television [and Digital] Culture at Royal Holloway[, University of London] and one of the editors of *Celebrity Studies*, acknowledges the negative side of the fame game, but believes it should no longer be simply reviled. He says: "Making more deliberative judgments in how we value, respond, and act on celebrity seems increasingly important."

We have learned much from Stephen Hawking about our universe. Now, perhaps, we can learn from him something important about ourselves.

"*We could all do more to identify the heroes living among us. They are our founders and builders. They lead us forward.*"

Too Many Celebrities, Not Enough Heroes

Landon Y. Jones

Landon Y. Jones was the managing editor of People *magazine from 1989 to 1997 and is the author of* William Clark and the Shaping of the West. *In the following viewpoint, he argues that the rise of the Internet and increasing reporting on the lives of celebrities have resulted in more and more interest in celebrities and less and less interest in real heroes. He says people are interested in celebrity failures or weaknesses, but are often put off when heroes have flaws. He worries that focusing on celebrities instead of heroes robs people of inspiration to be better human beings.*

As you read, consider the following questions:

1. Who is Richard Phillips, and how does Jones say his heroism has been questioned?

2. How does Jones say that Betty Ford contributed to the rise of celebrity culture?

3. According to Jones, what were Nelson Mandela's flaws?

Is Tom Hanks more or less worthy of our admiration than the man he portrays in *Captain Phillips*?

Tom Hanks vs. Richard Phillips

Hanks will head down the red carpet this weekend [in February 2014] with his film up for six Academy Awards, including best picture. He's already a two-time Oscar winner and the youngest recipient of the American Film Institute's Life Achievement Award. Astronomers named an asteroid in his honor after *Apollo 13*. The U.S. Army Ranger Hall of Fame inducted him as an honorary member after *Saving Private Ryan*. Polls peg him as the most likable man in Hollywood and the most trusted man in America.

Richard Phillips, meanwhile, has been hailed as a hero and honored at the White House—and immortalized by Hanks on film. But questions linger about how heroic he actually was when Somali pirates hijacked his container ship and held him hostage in April 2009. While the movie portrays him as a modest merchant mariner who kept his crew safe and remained quick-thinking throughout the ordeal, some real-life crewmates describe him as "arrogant" and accuse him of ignoring warnings and taking unnecessary risks. That scene in the movie where he offers himself to the pirates? ("If you're gonna shoot somebody, shoot me!") They say it didn't happen.

So do we throw our allegiances behind the celebrity or the potentially flawed hero? There was a time when we didn't have to choose; when our celebrities and our heroes tended to be one and the same. People became famous for great deeds. Think [first U.S. president] George Washington, [inventor] Thomas Edison, [pilot] Amelia Earhart, [astronaut] Neil Armstrong. But celebrity and heroism went their separate ways some time ago. It's become easier to obtain celebrity status, harder to be a hero. And when celebrity worship goes up against hero worship, the celebrities usually win.

That will be true at this year's Oscars. The theme of the show is "a celebration of movie heroes," the producers say. Yet even as our movie stars honor worthy heroes, the spotlight inevitably shines on the celebrities themselves.

The Rise of Celebrity Culture

I witnessed, and at times enthusiastically abetted, the multiple G-force rise of celebrity culture during my 23 years as a staffer and eventually managing editor at *People* magazine. *People* published its first issue on March 4, 1974—40 years ago this week—and I joined as an overworked junior writer a few weeks later.

The cover of that first issue had an Old Hollywood look. It featured Mia Farrow, dressed in gauzy white, her hair in pin curls, portraying Daisy Buchanan in *The Great Gatsby*. It was remarkably similar to how Farrow's mother, actress Maureen O'Sullivan, had appeared on the cover of *Film Pictorial* in 1933. But we quickly learned that our culture's fascination with celebrities had changed since Hollywood's golden era. Readers were more interested in Mia Farrow the woman, mother and personality than in Mia Farrow the actress. That first issue of *People* didn't even sell enough copies to make its advertising rate–base guarantee, though the article inside, written by F. Scott Fitzgerald's daughter, included the salacious tidbit that Farrow "became pregnant during the production (which would bring her a fourth child under the age of 4), and I heard there was some talk of an abortion." Readers were assured that for Farrow, "that idea would have been unthinkable."

What the public felt entitled to know about the lives of famous people, and what the news media felt entitled to report, expanded in the wake of Watergate [the scandal that forced President Richard Nixon to resign]. [President] Gerald and Betty Ford took up residence in the White House that August [1974], and a month later the new first lady received a breast cancer diagnosis. She spoke frankly about it to the news media, inviting photographers to take pictures of her in her hospital room, wearing a housecoat. "Radical mastectomy," *People* wrote in October 1974. "Suddenly, in the aftermath of Betty Ford's surgery, millions of Americans knew what it meant." Ford rewrote the script not just for first ladies but for all public figures. In a 1975 interview with *60 Minutes*, she said she wouldn't be surprised or especially concerned to hear that her daughter, then 18, was having premarital sex. During a televised White House tour, she noted that she and the president shared the same bed, and she told *McCall's* that she slept with her husband "as often as possible." Eventually, she would talk about her alcohol and painkiller addictions. For Ford, private problems were nothing to be embarrassed about. Opening up about them was honest, healthy, potentially inspiring.

For the news media, it was a short leap from covering Ford's cooperative candor to bringing more private lives into public view. If celebrities didn't want their problems turned into public fodder, too bad. It was the duty of the press to be accurate about the lives of the rich and famous. And readers demanded to be inspired and moved, but also titillated and amused.

Celebrity Covers Sell

As editor of *People*, I struggled to balance the magazine's dual mission: telling the stories of extraordinary people and the stories of ordinary people who did extraordinary things. Covers showcasing bona fide heroes—say, the first responders to the 1989 San Francisco earthquake or young mothers in the military who were mobilized during the Persian Gulf War— languished on newsstands. We had to rely on celebrity covers to make our circulation goals. And so I oversaw, in consecutive years, the anointment of Sean Connery, Tom Cruise, Patrick Swayze, Nick Nolte, Brad Pitt, Denzel Washington and George Clooney as the sexiest men alive. I published a complete guide to the O.J. Simpson trial and photographs of a nearly naked Demi Moore. Yes, we admire heroes, but we are mesmerized by celebrities. When Václav Havel met Paul Newman in 1990, the revered Czech leader marveled that the actor was "such a big legend that I didn't believe he physically exists."

It can be thrilling to be near celebrity's white-hot flame—even if we don't always know exactly why it's thrilling. On separate occasions, I interviewed two of the most famous women in the world: [actress] Elizabeth Taylor and Princess Diana [of Britain]. I still remember nervously dropping my tape recorder on the floor of Taylor's Bel Air home. Both encounters were fascinating. In the end, though, the strongest impression both women left me with was of their fragility.

Learning about the frailties of movie stars, rock stars, sports superstars and royals can humanize them. We gain a seeming intimacy that makes us comfortable judging them. When I first interviewed [then first lady] Hillary Clinton, in 1992, I brought along the newest issue of *People*. Princess Diana was on the cover, with a story about her troubled marriage. "Oh, I *knew* she married too young!" Clinton exclaimed.

But the tell-all era has been harder on heroes than on celebrities. We have less tolerance for flaws in our heroes. It is as if we measure them by entertainment values. The story lines we assign to them want excitement and triumph, but do not allow for the inconsistencies and failings the Greeks knew we all have. We struggle to reconcile the shining image of [South African human rights leader] Nelson Mandela with his quick temper, multiple marriages and often-discomforting political alliances. The flaw the public is least likely to forgive is lack of

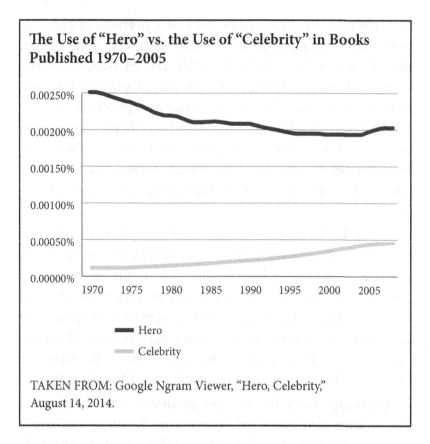

The Use of "Hero" vs. the Use of "Celebrity" in Books
Published 1970–2005

TAKEN FROM: Google Ngram Viewer, "Hero, Celebrity,"
August 14, 2014.

candor; good-bye, Lance Armstrong [a professional cyclist who admitted to using performance-enhancing drugs].

And so we end up with a scarcity of universally accepted public heroes amid an overabundance of celebrities.

Proliferating Celebrities

At the same time, the Internet and the constantly churning news cycle have eliminated the need for media gatekeepers to determine who will be made famous. There is a thriving international marketplace for proliferating celebrities. And high demand has generated even higher supply, along with a kind of Gresham's law of fame: Just as bad money drives out the good, celebrities are crowding out heroes.

To visualize this phenomenon, go to Google Ngram [Viewer] and plot the yearly count of the words "hero" and "celebrity" in books published since 1970. The word "hero" is on a steady down slope, while "celebrity" is rising rapidly.

You can also see the result of this trend on the landing page of *People*'s online archive of its covers. The category "real people" is dominated by crime victims and reality-show stars. Finding more stirringly heroic real people, such as Captain Chesley Sullenberger, the pilot of the US Airways flight that safely crash-landed in the Hudson River, requires searching the database.

Or check out the Pew Research Center's 2007 survey of millennials. When asked whom they most admire, a heartening number of them mentioned people close to them. Yet they were almost twice as likely to cite entertainers as they were to mention political figures. And compared with older cohorts, they were more likely to have entertainers and much less likely to have political, religious or business leaders at the top of the list.

I used to hear a variation on the most-admired question when I attended focus groups to find out what *People* readers were interested in. "Who are your heroes?" the moderators would ask as they warmed up the groups. But about a decade ago, they stopped asking about heroes. "They can't think of any," one moderator explained to me.

Perhaps that's because today's definition of "heroes" is drawn so narrowly. To find them, we tend to default to the military or superheroes, or to great figures in history.

After I retired from *People*, I chose to write about a historical hero: William Clark of the Lewis and Clark expedition. He was appealing, in part, because he was unencumbered by publicity agents or smoking-gun e-mails. Several of my friends among recovering weekly magazine editors have done the same, including Walter Isaacson of *Time* (Benjamin Franklin,

Albert Einstein), Jim Gaines of *Time* (Johann Sebastian Bach, Frederick the Great) and Evan Thomas of *Newsweek* (Dwight Eisenhower, John Paul Jones).

But we could all do more to identify the heroes living among us. They are our founders and builders. They lead us forward. They encourage us to stop thinking only about ourselves and our narrow interests and to think about a larger purpose.

Many celebrities do take on worthy causes. As the joke goes, a movie star without a cause is like a woodpecker without a tree. But celebrities do not typically help us to better understand ourselves and our world. They are more likely to reinforce our preconceptions than to lead us to new ideas.

So as we settle in to watch the Academy Awards on Sunday night, we can admire the parade of celebrities on the red carpet with a shiver of guilty pleasure. But it's also worth remembering that, as [poet] John Milton wrote about Lycidas, "Fame is no plant that grows on mortal soil." We'll need to look elsewhere for people who help us bridge the gap between who we are and who we want to be.

"As long as people are famous, people will have opinions and feelings and desires to be just like them or to be nothing like them ever. And that's okay."

Celebrity Culture Is Not That Terrible

Courtney Enlow

Courtney Enlow is the features editor at Pajiba. In the following viewpoint, she says that people love to follow celebrities, either to hate them or to empathize with them. She says that this is inevitable, and that while it is somewhat repulsive, it ultimately does little harm. She concludes that people should stop following celebrities if they can or want to, but if they cannot or find it enjoyable to follow celebrity culture, they should not worry about it too much.

As you read, consider the following questions:

1. What does Enlow say is the most obvious sign of celebrity culture "disease"?

2. Why does Enlow say non-celebrities can't understand celebrities?

3. What wish regarding celebrities does Enlow say will never come true?

Weekly, often twice weekly, I receive comments, tweets and street dance-off requests berating me for my frequent and harsh judgments. But I can't help it. I'M SICK. I am among those affected by the disease called "Celebrity Culture." I have spent 26 years under an onslaught of information regarding the highly unnatural world of fame, and it has ruined me. And probably you, too.

Or, I'm just an asshole. It's really an either/or scenario.

Signs of Celebrity Culture Disease

1. Universal schadenfreude

The most obvious sign of illness. Dear heavens, do we love the misfortune of others. The harder they fall, the harder our schadenfreude-rection. You think you're too cool? You think you're immune? Look at the explosion over this Weiner incident [in which Congressman Anthony Weiner was discovered to have sent indecent photos to women].

Ignoring any and all reaction you had to the real episode, now pretend it was [former Alaska governor] Sarah Palin. You would all look at the photos. And about 80% of you would laugh. Yes, there would be other emotions or thoughts mixed in there, but you know that the majority of you would enjoy that something bad happened to this person who irritates you.

To a much lesser extent, that is what happens during every celebrity scandal. Whether we actively "enjoy" it or not, we pay attention. Our interest is piqued by this bad thing that is happening to someone wealthier and more attractive than we are, and an ugly, ugly piece of us somehow feels they deserve the bad for all the good they've received.

2. Voyeurism as sport

Public interest is not limited to the bad experiences in the life of a well-known individual. We are captivated by the good as well. To some, this may be a step in the right direction, a more positive spin on the last paragraph. But it isn't. Because we are still focusing time, energy and thought on something that has nothing to do with us.

This is of course at its clearest in the realm of reality television, particularly those that follow the famous and semi-famous in their regular day-to-day, made-for-television lives. Have you watched a Kardashian show [referring to *Keeping Up with the Kardashians*, a reality TV show]? Nothing happens. Ever. It's fake, scripted and it's still boring. . . . And yet people watch by the millions.

It's not merely limited to reality TV, though. Do a You-Tube search of absolutely any celebrity couple. Someone somewhere has made a tribute video set to a cheesy love song filled with their photos. Even brand-new couples I still don't 100% buy. We feel somehow involved in the lives of these strangers. Do you even know how many death threats [stripper Michelle] Bombshell McGee and [television personality] Jesse James received after they had their hookups behind the back of [James's wife, actress] Sandra Bullock? Somewhere between a shit ton and eleven billion. Sandy B. was hurt; we were all hurt.

Superiority and Inferiority

3. Superiority epidemic . . .

Ever notice how we all seem to know exactly how we'd behave in the same situations as these people of whose lives we have little to no comprehension?

To me, it's not dissimilar to the way of thinking about God. To ascribe human emotions like anger or pleasure to this being who, if even it exists, we are physically incapable of even imagining, is pointless. We do this same thing with those in the realm of fame. And to anyone who is horrified and/or amused that I just made a comparison between our Lord and a Jennifer Love Hewitt [an actress] or a Wilmer Valderrama [an actor], know that I did so because in the mind of a famous person, that makes perfect sense. We can't understand that level of delusion and ego, so we genuinely cannot understand any of the other shit they do.

4. . . . *with an inferiority virus outbreak*

And that's why, in addition to the aforementioned prettiness and wealth, we feel beneath them. It goes half and half—some of us fall at their feet, believing them to be better than we, some of us filled with hate towards these victims of sheer luck. For many of us, we have a couple of each, minimum. I know I do. [Actress Tilda] Swinton is a deity; [actor Ashton] Kutcher is a gnat that is constantly attempting to fly up my nose.

Either way, we know we're different from them, deserved or not.

"Who Cares?"

5. *A complete and total loss of empathy*

When [actress] Lindsay Lohan's fancy anklet [that is, her court-stipulated ankle monitor] starts going all beepy-buzzy, very few respond "that poor girl." More often than not, it's "that stupid bitch." We find them so different from us, the mere peons, we no longer treat these people as though they are in any way human. They are things, rag dolls paid to dance around for our enjoyment and disdain, depending on what we desire that day.

My response to every commenter in the history of the Internet who says, "Who cares?" is this: people. People care. They do. I wish they didn't, I wish I didn't, but I do. That's the culture.

And that's okay. Because at the end of the day, it doesn't matter.

How is it affecting your life if your office mates pore over *People* magazine with intensity? Is it really the worst thing in the world that people really give a shit about whether or not [actress] Jennifer Aniston is still all broken up about [actor and former husband] Brad Pitt? . . . It's the circle of fame. They exist, and it is that enjoyment and disdain that keeps them there. Some of it is too much, some of it is awful, and some of it, when done in a manner that actually disrupts people's lives . . . should be examined. But for the rest of us, let's just carry on. Because as long as people are famous, people will have opinions and feelings and desires to be just like them or to be nothing like them ever. And that's okay.

Like everyone else, I too get worried that [reality TV] shows like *Teen Mom* and *Jersey Shore* are leading to dipshit teenagers actively trying to be famous for the same reasons the people on those programs are. But then I remember something: No, they aren't. And if they are, they have way bigger problems than cable television, and they'd probably be f---ups anyway. They're someone else's problem, and we're far too busy with other, more famous people who aren't our problem.

I wish we could all be goodly people, unaffected by a twisted fascination with the rich and famous. But that's a wish that will never come true. So, we laugh and point at the monkeys with the cymbals and enjoy the show.

Be a better person if you can be. Otherwise, hate on, haters. You're doing your part to keep the circle unbroken.

"The new public service announcements encourage men to speak up and step in if they see someone in danger of being sexually assaulted."

Celebrities Work to Prevent Sexual Assault

Lesley Clark and Renee Schoof

Lesley Clark is the White House correspondent for McClatchy's Washington bureau; Renee Schoof covers education, colleges, job training, and special education for McClatchy. In the following viewpoint, they report on White House efforts to reduce sexual assault and rape on college campuses. They report that these efforts include initiating surveys to identify the scope of the problem on college campuses, working to prevent assaults, and working to make schools respond more effectively to reports of sexual assault. They further explain that the White House has also launched a campaign featuring male celebrities condemning sexual assault and urging other men to intervene when they see such violence taking place.

As you read, consider the following questions:

1. According to the White House report, how many women are sexually assaulted in college?

2. According to the viewpoint, what does Daniel Craig say in his public service spot?

3. What types of questions are asked in the eighteen-page White House survey sent to colleges?

The [Barack] Obama administration on Tuesday [in April 2014] unveiled a celebrity public service announcement, a new website, NotAlone.gov, and a series of recommendations aimed at lowering the alarming rate of sexual assaults on college campuses.

Facing Up to Sexual Assault on Campus

The action came as Vice President Joe Biden said officials at colleges and universities, even if they fear their schools' reputations may be damaged, "can no longer turn a blind eye and pretend rape and sexual assault don't occur on their campuses."

"Colleges and universities need to face the fact of what exists on their campuses," Biden said. "They need to step up to it."

The first report of the White House Task Force to Protect Students from Sexual Assault estimates that one in five women are sexually assaulted while in college, most often in their freshman or sophomore years. In the majority of cases, it's by someone the woman knows, and most often women don't report what happened.

Biden, who was introduced by a woman who was assaulted at Harvard University, said only 13 percent of women attacked report the crime to their schools.

"They fear they'll be shamed. They're embarrassed," he said. "Or scared they won't be safe on campus with their attacker roaming around or maybe sitting in the same history class."

The steps include identifying the scope of the problem on individual college campuses, helping prevent assaults, helping schools respond effectively and making the federal government's enforcement efforts more transparent. The recommendations were put forward after three months of 27 sessions with more than 2,000 people who made suggestions.

The administration plans to hold more listening sessions and revise the report. One theme from the sessions was that it was too hard for students who are victims of sexual crimes to find information about how to report them, said Tina Tchen, executive director of the White House Council on Women and Girls.

"We need to provide survivors with more support and we need to bring perpetrators to justice," Biden said.

The website will make enforcement data public and make other resources accessible to students and schools. Students can learn about their rights, search enforcement data and read about how to file a complaint. It also will provide schools and advocates with federal guidance on legal obligations. The site also features resources from outside the federal government, such as hotline numbers and mental health services locatable with a zip code.

The Department of Education will release new guidance clarifying that on-campus counselors and advocates can talk to survivors in confidence. Biden said the task force heard from too many schools that believed counselors could not maintain confidentiality.

Actors Speak Out

The administration also wants to bring men into the equation. It released public service announcements featuring President Barack Obama, Biden and actors Daniel Craig, Seth Meyers, Benicio Del Toro, Steve Carell and Dule Hill.

"We've got to send a message to men everywhere, you've got to be part of the solution," Biden said. Women must give verbal consent, he said: "Everything else is rape and assault."

The new public service announcements encourage men to speak up and step in if they see someone in danger of being sexually assaulted. "If I saw it happening, I'd never blame her. I'd help her," Craig says in the spot.

Biden called on schools to conduct a campus climate survey to gauge the prevalence of sexual assault and student awareness of the problem. The administration plans to make the campus climate surveys mandatory in 2016.

The administration also will provide training for school officials who are involved in investigating and adjudicating sexual assault cases.

"It's great to see the White House really putting a lot of effort into this issue," said Andrea Pino, a University of North Carolina [UNC] at Chapel Hill student who, with former UNC student Annie Clark, were among those who filed a complaint about the handling of sexual assault cases against their university.

A separate complaint accused the university of noncompliance with the federal Clery Act [the Jeanne Clery Disclosure of Campus Security Policy and Campus Crime Statistics Act], which requires universities that receive federal aid to collect and disclose information about crime that occurs on and near campus. The cases are under federal investigation.

Pino and Clark also helped found a national advocacy network. "It's inspiring to see advocates here of different generations and seeing unity on this issue," Pino said. "There's a lot more to do. This is a first step."

Clark said the policies aren't "exactly where we want them yet." Advocates will continue to work with the federal government, she said. One major problem is that the Department of

Education doesn't have the funding and staffing to handle the complaints it's receiving and isn't enforcing the law, she said.

A task force at UNC–Chapel Hill has been meeting for more than a year to rewrite the university's sexual assault and harassment policies. The group has hashed out the structure of the adjudication process along with sanctions and grounds for appeal. Recommendations to Chancellor Carol Folt are expected soon.

A university spokeswoman said Tuesday that UNC-CH commends the White House for "making this important issue a priority, and we share their passion for providing safer campuses for our students."

Folt was one of about a dozen university leaders who attended the White House meeting on Tuesday. She also attended a listening session of the White House task force in February.

North Carolina students also met with the group led by Biden, including a graduate student from UNC-CH and a student from North Carolina Central University.

Campus Climate Surveys

The White House effort will elevate the issue "in a way that will get the attention of college campuses across the country," said Sen. Claire McCaskill, D-Mo., who has been championing efforts to combat sexual assaults and who attended the event. "This is a complex and difficult problem," said McCaskill, a former county prosecutor. "The more people who put their shoulder to this effort, the more progress we're going to make."

The campus climate surveys will show how students feel about their safety and whether they think rape cases are being handled appropriately. McCaskill is working on a separate survey of 450 schools that will give a statistically valid sample of what all schools are doing to address the problem of campus rape.

The White House Report on Campus Sexual Assault

One in five women is sexually assaulted in college. Most often, it's by someone she knows—and also most often, she does not report what happened. Many survivors are left feeling isolated, ashamed or to blame. Although it happens less often, men, too, are victims of these crimes.

The president created the Task Force to Protect Students from Sexual Assault to turn this tide. As the name of our new website—NotAlone.gov—indicates, we are here to tell sexual assault survivors that they are not alone. And we're also here to help schools live up to their obligation to protect students from sexual violence. . . .

We are providing schools with a tool kit to conduct a survey—and we urge schools to show they're serious about the problem by conducting the survey next year. . . .

Prevention programs can change attitudes, behavior—and the culture. In addition to identifying a number of promising prevention strategies that schools can undertake now, we are also researching new ideas and solutions. But one thing we know for sure: We need to engage men as allies in this cause. Most men are not perpetrators—and when we empower men to step in when someone's in trouble, they become an important part of the solution.

White House Task Force to Protect Students from Sexual Assault,
"Not Alone: The First Report of the White House Task Force
to Protect Students from Sexual Assault," April 2014.

The 18-page surveys include questions about how colleges and universities report and investigate rapes and sexual assaults and what the institutions do to help victims of these crimes. The surveys were sent out over the past few weeks.

McCaskill said individual schools' responses would be kept confidential to encourage candid responses. Data from the surveys showing the extent of campus sexual assault would be released after a series of meetings beginning in May, she said. McCaskill also plans to work on a new law that clarifies existing laws and "makes it simpler for universities to do the right thing," she said.

She planned to hold hearings in the summer and get a draft of the bill prepared before the school year starts. The report's recommendations drew praise from across the aisle, as well.

Rep. Patrick Meehan, R-Pa., called it a "vital step forward" in efforts to keep students on college campuses safe.

"These recommendations will help victims navigate the reporting process, enhance transparency in federal enforcement efforts and help schools build community partnerships with organizations like rape crisis centers that provide critical services for victims," Meehan said.

> *"How many of [Miley] Cyrus's young fans will interpret her behavior as a normal part of growing up? How many will confuse lasciviousness with sexual maturity?"*

Why Miley Cyrus Matters

Mona Charen

Mona Charen is a syndicated columnist and author of Do-Gooders: How Liberals Hurt Those They Claim to Help (and the Rest of Us). *In the following viewpoint, she argues that pop star Miley Cyrus's lewd performance at the 2013 MTV Video Music Awards is a new low in pop culture and may be damaging to children. She points out that Cyrus used images of childhood, including teddy bears, in a sexual way, which Charen says legitimizes and normalizes child pornography and child sexual abuse.*

As you read, consider the following questions:

1. According to Charen, on what basis does Cyrus make judgments?

2. How does Meghan Cox Gurdon say that violent children's books damage children?

3. How did Cyrus originally become a sensation, according to Charen?

Some defenders of [singer] Miley Cyrus's VMA [MTV Video Music Award] performance [which many considered overly sexual] don't understand what all the outrage is about. [Singer] Justin Timberlake tweeted, "She's young. Take it easy on her." [Actor and writer] Lena Dunham worried about "slut shaming." [Businessman] Russell Simmons wrote, "Just saw @MileyCyrus. What did I miss. She was having fun. #twerkmileytwerk." And [singer] Adam Lambert tweeted, "Listen if it wasn't ur cup of tea—all good but why is everyone spazzing? Hey—she's doin something right. We all talkin."

Undermining Good Taste

Cyrus seemed to endorse Lambert's any-attention-is-good-attention rationale. She boasted on Twitter, "Smilers! My VMA performance had 306,000 tweets per minute. That's more than the blackout or Superbowl! #fact."

Doubtless if Cyrus had undressed completely and performed a literal (rather than pantomime) sex act on stage, her Twitter numbers would have been even higher. Ditto if she had twisted the head off a small animal or defecated live and in color. A product of the celebrity culture, she seems incapable of making judgments based on anything higher than buzz. If she did either of those things, would Lambert wonder why everyone was "spazzing" and would Dunham condemn "slut shaming"? It's hard to say.

How many of Cyrus's young fans will interpret her behavior as a normal part of growing up? How many will confuse lasciviousness with sexual maturity?

Meghan Cox Gurdon, the *Wall Street Journal*'s wise children's book reviewer, noted in a recent Hillsdale College speech that there is a vein in "young adult" fiction of ugly, horrific, and sexually revolting material aimed at kids between twelve and 18. Girls cut themselves with razors until their bellies are a "mess of meat and blood," and boys don magic glasses that reveal "impaled heads and other black-rot body parts: hands, hearts, feet, ears, penises." The authors and publishers justify these themes as "heartbreakingly honest."

The subversives who undermine good taste always seem to invoke "honesty" or "reality." But as Gurdon rightly objects: "Books tell children what to expect, what life is, what culture is, how we are expected to behave—what the spectrum is. They form norms. . . . And teenagers are all about identifying norms and adhering to them."

No one who has ever observed a group of 15-year-old girls—nearly identical in their hair styles, clothes, and speech—can doubt this.

Miley Cyrus's performance was not just another case of a salacious and degrading bid for attention. Because of who she was—a Disney star with a loyal following of young girls—and because of what she did, she has introduced something even darker to the mainstream culture. She is indirectly legitimizing child porn.

Promoting Sexual Abuse

Miley Cyrus became a sensation as "Hannah Montana," a wholesome Disney pop star. Millions of preteen girls adored the show and followed Cyrus's career. She is hardly the first celebrity to attempt to shock her audience by shedding her ingénue image. Britney Spears, Lindsay Lohan, and others have plowed this ground. But Cyrus did more than cast off her innocence. She used innocence itself as a lecherous come-on.

Cyrus, 20, began her vulgar dance by appearing in a teddy bear costume, with dancing teddy bears as backup. She later exchanged this for a flesh-colored bra and panties and a large foam finger that she put to lewd uses.

I haven't ever seen child porn, but I would bet that a great deal of it uses images of innocence and childhood—like teddy bears—for the delectation of its audience. Cyrus has now taken this perversion mainstream.

Child porn, like every other kind of pornography, once relegated to a seedy underworld, is now as close as a cell phone. It's bobbing along in the twilight, close to the surface of American lives, but kept from full view by the last remaining shreds of propriety that our culture enforces.

The existence of the Internet has probably already eroded some of the shame that pedophiles once felt. Learning that hundreds of thousands of others share one's perversion must be cathartic. But how much more liberating to see the themes of child sexual abuse portrayed approvingly at the VMA awards?

American popular culture continues to prove that there is no rock bottom, and everyone who shrugs that it's no big deal is a little bit complicit.

> "The vast majority of food and drink endorsements of elite professional athletes were full of sugar or calories without healthy nutrients."

Celebrities Promote Unhealthy Eating and Obesity

Tara Haelle

Tara Haelle is a reporter at the Chicago Bureau, a news website that focuses on issues that matter to young people. In the following viewpoint, Haelle reports on a study showing that celebrity athletes overwhelmingly endorse products that are full of sugar and empty calories. She says advertisements for these products are targeted at teens. The exact effect of such advertisements is unclear, she maintains, though it is known that teens recognize the celebrities and can identify the messages they are supposed to be receiving. She concludes that researchers are hopeful that over time more people will become aware of the dangers of these kinds of celebrity endorsements and that celebrities will come under pressure to endorse healthier foods.

As you read, consider the following questions:

1. What percentage of athlete endorsements consisted of food and beverages, according to a Yale study?

2. According to the viewpoint, which age groups saw the most celebrity endorsement ads for foods?

3. Why doesn't Yoni Freedhoff think that conversations in classrooms or at home can undo the effect of celebrity endorsements?

Concerns about teen and childhood obesity have topped public health priorities in the past several years, with programs such as First Lady Michelle Obama's "Let's Move!" campaign aiming to encourage more healthful behaviors. But recent research suggests that one of the biggest obstacles to progress might be campaigns of a more ubiquitous nature—ads featuring unhealthy food and drink endorsements by celebrities.

Unhealthy

A study published last fall [in 2013] found that the vast majority of food and drink endorsements of elite professional athletes were full of sugar or calories without healthy nutrients. And it was teens who saw these ads the most. The study, published in *Pediatrics* in October by researchers at Yale University's Rudd Center for Food Policy and Obesity, led to more in-depth research to learn about the effects of these ads on kids and teens.

According to the Yale study, professional athletes' endorsements of food and beverages made up about a quarter of all their endorsements in 2010, second only to sporting goods and apparel. Yet, approximately four out of every five food products endorsed by influential athletes that year were high-calorie and nutrient-poor. Further, added sugar accounted for all the calories in just over 93 percent of the drinks endorsed by the athletes.

Not that these findings are surprising, according to Yoni Freedhoff, MD, an obesity specialist and assistant professor of family medicine at the University of Ottawa.

"The least surprising aspect of the study's findings are that the athletes as a whole are endorsing the worst foods our food industry has to offer," Freedhoff said. "Those foods that are the least nutritious are also the food industry's biggest profit drivers. The food industry's sole responsibility is to maximize profit, and celebrities and athletes help them do so."

The Yale study analyzed the endorsements in TV, radio, newspapers and magazines of the top 100 professional athletes based on their prominence and endorsement value as ranked by *Bloomberg Businessweek* in 2010. Together, the athletes had endorsed 122 food and drink brands that year, but 79 percent of the endorsed food products had few nutrients and high calorie counts, and nearly all the drinks had nothing but sugar calories added. Leading the pack in unhealthy food endorsements that year were football player Peyton Manning, basketball player LeBron James and tennis player Serena Williams. The two athletes with the highest overall endorsements were Manning and baseball player Ryan Howard, but Howard, with 21 total advertisements, promoted Subway and Powerade whereas Manning's 25 advertisements were for Gatorade, Wheaties, Nabisco and Pepsi. Among the 13 advertisements with Williams were endorsements for Oreo, Gatorade, Nabisco 100-Calorie Snack Packs and the Got Milk? campaign. James promoted Sprite, Vitaminwater, McDonald's and Powerade.

"There's zero doubt the food industry gets a return on their investment," Freedhoff said. "Industry isn't in the business of throwing away money, and a return means that those endorsements generate more additional income than they cost to buy in the first place."

Targeting Teens

While it's not hard to find figures on endorsement deals or the value of individual celebrities, precise numbers on the amount the food and beverage industry spends on celebrity endorsements is hard to come by, as is research into the effectiveness of these endorsements. But if they are effective, there is less doubt about what audiences they are reaching.

The researchers analyzed Nielsen data to determine what age groups watched these athletes' food and drink commercials and found that teens aged 12 to 17 saw the most, an average 35 commercials during 2010. Adults saw an average 33 commercials with these athletes, and children under age 12 saw an average 21 commercials.

It was the second study, published this winter and sponsored by the WAT-AAH! Foundation and Fit Kids, which aimed to better understand the effect these celebrity endorsements had on children and teens. The study recruited 166 youth, aged 8 to 17, from seven major metropolitan areas to participate in one-hour focus groups. The kids all watched at least an hour of TV a day and regularly participated in sports or other physical activities.

After a discussion, the focus groups watched three to four commercials featuring a music or sports celebrity's endorsement of a food or drink. In the ads shown, products such as Pepsi, Gatorade, Sprite, McDonald's and Diet Coke were promoted by celebrities such as [singer] Beyoncé, [singer] Taylor Swift, LeBron James, Peyton Manning, [basketball player] Dwyane Wade and [tennis player] Maria Sharapova.

Many of these names had also come up during the preceding discussion when focus group participants listed their favorite celebrities. The participants said they admired these celebrities and wanted to be like them. . . .

Before watching the commercials shown during the study, the most remembered commercials among the participants included Gatorade, Coke, Pepsi, Sprite, Mountain Dew, and McDonald's, and the most remembered celebrities in commercials included Beyoncé, Taylor Swift, LeBron James, [rapper] Drake, [rapper] Lil Wayne, [singer] Michael Jackson, Peyton Manning and [basketball player] Michael Jordan.

"Health-Washing" Products

"There's no doubt," Freedhoff said, "especially with our children, that the presence of their heroes, heroes who themselves are the embodiment of physical fitness and health, serve to very clearly 'health-wash' the products they're shilling."

According to the focus group findings, the participating children and teens seemed aware of the ads' goals. "The respondents reported that the test commercials conveyed many desirable product benefits and attributes: improved performance, increased creativity, boost in confidence and success," the report noted. To the participants, "these ads developed by Pepsi, Sprite and Diet Coke were powerful especially because the commercials featured top celebrity names, catchy music and captured the celebrities' skills (dancing, basketball tricks and song writing), which were all easily recognizable to their demographic."

Yet the in-depth report offered a somewhat silver lining as well. While 77 percent of the participants initially believed the test commercials "were compelling and strongly encouraged consumption and/or purchase intent," just under a quarter of them (23 percent) still felt that way after discussing the ads' objectives, the believability of their messages and the health effects of the featured products.

Endorse Fruits and Vegetables

In other words, the participants recognized that the products were unhealthy "junk food" and found it hard to believe that healthy, active celebrities were actually eating and drinking those products. As they discussed the commercials, the participants called the ads and celebrities "misleading" or "dishonest" and said they felt deceived. Some participants called for the celebrities to stop endorsing such products and to instead endorse healthy foods such as fruits and vegetables.

Celebrity Endorsement

One of the most popular advertising techniques world-wide is to have a celebrity endorse a product. Celebrity endorsement is usually only a part, but an important part, of a larger product marketing campaign. In addition to being well known and famous, celebrities are attractive, likeable, and trustworthy—at least in the minds of the public to whom the advertising message is directed. The hope is that the celebrities' qualities will be "transferred" in some way to a product and stimulate sales. Advertisers avoid celebrities, such as [football player] O.J. Simpson, who have negative reputations. However, very little research has been done on the issue of celebrity endorsement. Scholars have discovered only a few things of note. One important finding is that celebrity endorsement is culture specific, that is, celebrity endorsement is most effective in the celebrity's home country. For example, an American celebrity endorsing a product in an advertisement broadcast in Austria was less effective in fostering an intent to purchase than a non-celebrity native spokesperson, making the country of origin (COO) an important factor in endorsement decisions. Other scholars see celebrity endorsers as "cultural products" of their respective countries that are particularly effective if their countries are political and financial powers. In a capitalistic society, it just makes sense to use celebrities to sell products or services. Capitalism has always made maximum use of the tools it has available to pursue profit.

Larry Z. Leslie,
Celebrity in the 21st Century: A Reference Handbook.
Santa Barbara, CA: ABC-CLIO, 2011.

Freedhoff couldn't agree more. "I have yet to see a celebrity or an athlete promoting produce," he said. "Certainly as a society we need to be consuming far more produce and far fewer products." What is less clear is whether the shifts in these participants' perspectives will last beyond the one-hour focus groups, or whether similar discussions in homes or classrooms might change consumption habits of unhealthy foods and drinks.

Freedhoff doesn't think so. He suggested that the artificial setup of the study influenced participants to say what they knew they were expected to say, and one hour can hardly undo the power of these endorsements.

Selling Illness

"The impact of commercials on both adults and child alike goes far beyond the actual message and extends into emotional, unconscious brand association," he said. "Moreover, given their sheer volume, and even with wonderful media education, there is simply no way for anyone to regularly be on guard against advertising's messaging or impact."

There are not obvious or easy solutions, Freedhoff said. "Even if we take the findings at face value—that through engagement we can help children defend against the predatory nature of advertising—it rather tragically places the onus on children and educators to respond to a practice that, given the target population, can fairly be described as loathsome," he said.

Given how little research has been done in this area, though, it may be additional research that eventually makes the difference. "My hope," Freedhoff said, "is that this [Yale] research serves to highlight what has become an awful new normal—the normal of athletes selling illness to their most impressionable fans—and that over time, with continued exposure and finger-pointing, one day it will no longer be considered a smart career move to sell sugared sodas or junk food as a celebrity."

Periodical and Internet Sources Bibliography

The following articles have been selected to supplement the diverse views presented in this chapter.

Victoria Ahearn	"John Cusack Laments 'Madness' of Celebrity Culture; Points to Bieber Coverage," *Vancouver Sun*, September 10, 2014.
Stanley Crouch	"Sarah Palin, Kim Kardashian, and Our Poisonous Celebrity Culture: Shame, Fame, and the American Way," *New York Daily News*, December 20, 2010.
Katie Drummond	"Can Skinny Celebs Help Your Body Image?," *Prevention*, October 2012.
James Houran	"Is It—or Can It Be—Psychologically Beneficial to Follow Celebrity News?," *Science and Religion Today*, March 1, 2012.
Rae Mullins	"The Cult of Celebrity," *Huffington Post UK*, August 18, 2014.
George Packer	"Celebrating Inequality," *New York Times*, May 19, 2013.
Jo Piazza	"Americans Have an Unhealthy Obsession with Celebrities," *Huffington Post*, March 28, 2012.
Claire Schmidt	"Jennifer Lawrence to Lena Dunham: 15 Inspiring Celebrity Quotes About Body Image," Today.com, May 3, 2014.
Alexandra Sifferlin	"When Good Celebrities Promote Bad Foods," *Time*, October 7, 2013.
Jamie Tehrani	"Viewpoint: Did Our Brains Evolve to Foolishly Follow Celebrities?," BBC News, June 25, 2013.

OPPOSING
VIEWPOINTS®
SERIES

CHAPTER 2

Is Celebrity
Activism Beneficial?

Chapter Preface

A number of celebrity mothers have worked to promote breast-feeding, which is touted by pediatricians and health officials as the best way for mothers to supply their babies with essential nutrients, a nutritionally balanced meal, and disease-fighting antibodies that help protect infants from illness. Actress Olivia Wilde, for example, appeared breast-feeding her infant in a series of photographs in *Glamour* in August 2014. Other celebrities, including model Gisele Bündchen, actress Miranda Kerr, and singer Gwen Stefani, have also had public photos taken of themselves breast-feeding their children.

Amanda Marcotte in an August 6, 2014, post at the Daily Beast argues that celebrity photos of breast-feeding are positive. She notes, "it's always good to see breast-feeding normalized," since women are sometimes shamed for breast-feeding in public, and making breast-feeding acceptable gives all working mothers more options. "Having a little celebrity assistance is sure to help those efforts, and further quiet down the remaining voices that exclaim that there's something indecent about women breast-feeding in public."

Marcotte also argues that it is inspiring and important that celebrities are being shown breast-feeding while working. "These photos also push back on the still-persistent idea in our culture that women who become mothers should hang up everything else they are in order to build their entire identity around motherhood." She further adds that glamorous photos of celebrities breast-feeding demonstrate that women can be mothers and still be sexy and glamorous. She concludes that "we're always going to have celebrity and fashion media foisting impossibly beautiful fantasies on us, but at least those fantasies have something to do with the lives that we really want to be leading."

Other commenters have been more skeptical about the trend of celebrity breast-feeding images. Susan Rohwer in an August 2014 opinion piece in the *Los Angeles Times*, for example, argues that the images of the glamorous and beautiful breast-feeding tends to cover up the fact that the United States makes breast-feeding very difficult for most women: Maternal leave policies in the United States are much worse than those in other developed countries, and women are often prevented from breast-feeding in public. Rohwer also points out that celebrity glamour photos make breast-feeding look effortless, when for many mothers, breast-feeding is very difficult. "The hurdles that new moms face in trying to fulfill the extended breast-feeding recommendations put forth by health experts are something we rarely hear celebrities talk about." She concludes that "we could all stand to see a little less fantasy about motherhood and a little more reality." She suggests that instead of focusing on celebrities breast-feeding, it would be more helpful to women to have a realistic conversation about the difficulties of breast-feeding and how policies could be changed to make breast-feeding easier for non-celebrity, non-wealthy women.

The following chapter focuses on other kinds of celebrity activism, including celebrity philanthropy and celebrity endorsement of worthy causes.

> "Rather than try to suppress our love of celebrity, we ought to channel it in optimally intelligent and fruitful directions."

Celebrities Can Help Bring Attention to Worthy Causes

Alain de Botton

Alain de Botton is a philosopher and television presenter; he is the author of The News: A User's Manual. *In the following viewpoint, he argues that many people see admiring celebrities as childish or ridiculous. He says that, on the contrary, interest in celebrities is natural and can also be beneficial. He points to Angelina Jolie, an actress who has raised the profile of humanitarian crises in Africa. He concludes that society should work to elevate celebrities who do worthwhile things with their power rather than trying to avoid celebrities altogether.*

As you read, consider the following questions:

1. What does the author worry will happen if serious people decide that celebrity culture is beneath them?

2. According to the viewpoint, why are individuals not usually motivated by love of justice and humanitarian generosity?

3. What are some things that the author thinks society needs celebrities to make sexy?

The term "celebrity culture" does to celebrity what "materialism" does to shopping: dismisses the whole thing as banal and evil. The only way clever people do celebrity is ironically: the chosen approach of many a smart, biting columnist, who wants to let you know she too has been thinking of [singer] Harry Styles, but only ironically, thankfully (given the degree from Balliol [College]).

Admiration Is Natural

The elite implication is that there is something demeaning and childish about the need to hero-worship or dwell on a famous person who is our contemporary but who doesn't know us: It seems passive and inferior, a confession of inadequacy, a proof that we are insufficiently engaged with our own projects and have chosen to "escape" from our lives because we have no idea how to lead them properly.

This is a real pity—and problematic too, for if serious people judge the very concept of celebrity to be beneath them, then the role of anointing celebrities (which everyone can have a shot at doing, the *Guardian* as much as any other group with a constituency) will fall to organisations entirely untroubled by the prospect of appealing to the lowest denominator.

The impulse to admire is an ineradicable and important feature of our psyches. Ignoring or condemning it won't kill it off; it will simply force it underground, where it will lurk untended and undeveloped, prone to latch on to inappropriate targets. Rather than try to suppress our love of celebrity, we ought to channel it in optimally intelligent and fruitful direc-

Angelina Jolie

In the late 1990s, Angelina Jolie became one of the most intriguing actresses to hit the screen, thanks to some meaty roles and an off-stage image of being dark and wild. Thanks to quirks such as her knife collection and assortment of tattoos, she has cultivated a reputation for being edgy, and she possesses a raw sexuality that she does not hesitate to discuss in interviews. Jolie also displayed a maturity and a talent that has led her from playing everything from a drug-addled supermodel to an undercover agent. A large part of her appeal, undeniably, is her looks. . . .

Jolie used the fame she garnered early on to do good around the world. She was invited to be a goodwill ambassador to the United Nations and has pretty much traveled consistently since then, doing what she could to raise awareness of problems around the world. She was in Cambodia filming the movie *Lara Croft: Tomb Raider* when she became aware of the problems with mines in the area. She fell in love with the people and adopted a boy, Maddox, from the country. Not wanting her son to grow up not knowing his homeland, she bought a house in Cambodia and became a citizen of the country.

"Angelina Jolie," Biography in Context.
Detroit, MI: Gale, 2013.

tions. A properly organised society would be one where the best-known people were those who embodied and reinforced the highest, noblest and most socially beneficial values, and hence one in which an admission of reverence for a celebrity could be an occasion for pride rather than a prompt for shame or self-deprecating laughter.

Making Worthy Causes "Sexy"

Last year [2013], Angelina Jolie was the highest-paid female star in Hollywood. She goes to Africa a lot, too. She doesn't visit refugee camps in the Democratic Republic of the Congo or in Rwanda to boost her income. She goes there to help people who are in great need. But more than anything, what she does is make Africa "sexy".

This is often seen as ridiculous—and a key reason why we should despise celebrities. A moralistic, or aggressively "mature" person would point out that we should not need celebrity endorsement to get worried about systematic rape or the plight of refugees in Sierra Leone or Tanzania. That's true. But in reality such attitudes are self-defeating. They fatally miscalculate what it takes to motivate people.

In a fantasy world we'd be motivated purely by the love of justice and humanitarian generosity. But most of us are not like that. We need a lot of encouragement, a lot of inducements, before we direct our thoughts—and money and effort—to distant strangers. Not because we are mean but because we are normal. It's normal to care a lot more about your own family than about other people's, to be obsessed about your own life and pretty detached about the suffering of people you'll never meet. Getting over that hurdle isn't simple, though sometimes it's important. The stern moralist forgets the barrier is there and so can't help us over it.

Something—a place or a cause—becomes "sexy" when we are given a sense that enthusiasm for it would be understood and liked by some very exciting people. By buying into it, we position ourselves as a little more attractive and glamorous. Jolie helps us to feel good about ourselves for caring about things that actually do deserve our concern, but which are at risk of seeming so miserable and intractable that we would otherwise simply tune out.

What Jolie does with Africa can be done with many other things. We need celebs to make a whole lot else sexy, including reading, being kind, forgiving and working towards social justice. Ideally, it would be normal for the most captivating people to lend their magnetism to the promotion of our best, long-term interests. Too often at present, fame and sex appeal are given over exclusively to profit seeking. The things we genuinely need have not as yet been able, or willing, to draw on the raw appeal of the most glamorous and most famous people on the planet.

We are used to thinking that anyone who "copies" a celebrity is sad and inauthentic, but in its highest form, imitation founded on admiration is integral to a good life. To refuse to admire, to take no interest in what distinguished others are up to, is to shut ourselves off, grandly and implausibly, from important knowledge. The job of the news is to make the celebrity section no less exciting than it is now, while ensuring that it provides us with portraits of people who can guide us to what matters, in ourselves and the world.

| *"You can't speak authoritatively against corporate and economic oppression if you're a wealthy glamour-boy."*

Celebrities Make Worthy Causes Absurd

Douglas Valentine

Douglas Valentine is the author of numerous books, including The Phoenix Program. *In the following viewpoint, he argues that celebrities make any cause they endorse absurd. Celebrities, he says, do not promote or help the causes with which they associate themselves. Instead, he argues, celebrities inadvertently trivialize important issues by endorsing them.*

As you read, consider the following questions:

1. What causes has Russell Brand taken up, according to Valentine?

2. How does Valentine say that Glenn Greenwald rendered himself absurd?

3. Why does Valentine believe that the "powers that be" thank Russell Brand?

Russell Brand is a celebrity, one of those pretty faces you see on ragged magazines at the checkout counter and think: "Who gives a flying f what he's screwing this week?"

Glitz and Principle

At one point he was screwing Katy Perry, a teeny-bopper who makes recruitment music videos for the US Army. They were married in a traditional Hindu ceremony, near a tiger sanctuary in India—which is just so cool! Except they divorced a year later, right after Brand, the cad, Twittered an unflattering photo of Perry for all their fans to see.

Brand meditates, but prefers transcendental medication. According to Wikipedia, he "has incorporated his notorious drug use, alcoholism, and promiscuity into his comedic material." And he certainly has a talent for casting himself as a rebel (there's a poster of him floating around the Internet depicting him as [revolutionary fighter] Che Guevara) and for shameless self-promotion: something of a serial flasher, he's been arrested numerous times, often, ironically, for throwing punches at paparazzo.

On Facebook he is adored by millions of millennial girls for his "gorgeous beard" and for being a vegetarian, which equals a reverence for all sentient beings. And yet, simply because he's a celebrity, he must constantly defend himself from charges of being "trivial," which really hurts when you're a sensitive guy like Brand.

And he is sensitive, and has convictions, as well as arrests. Brand has publicly condemned Israel's assault on Gaza and the "cruel and massive loss of life of the citizens of Gaza." He has taken other principled stands as well.

But he drenched himself in glitz, and acted like a fool, to get to the point where people would look at him and listen to what he says. And that is the irony of Brand's karma-challenged life: He suffers for the fame and fortune he brought upon himself.

© Scott Metzger, "Take a look at the chart and tell me your pain level on a scale of 1 to 10," Cartoonstock.com.

Don't you get it, Russ? You can't speak authoritatively against corporate and economic oppression if you're a wealthy glamour-boy, featured regularly in *GQ* and *Esquire*.

This is the trap all our modern heroes fall into. The first (paraphrased) words [activist and military analyst] Dan Ellsberg spoke to me were: "You can't understand me because you're not a celebrity. Being a celebrity changes everything."

Danny was absolutely right. Being a celebrity does change everything. Ask [Robert Allen] Zimmerman, [that is, singer Bob Dylan] who stopped pretending to be a champion of the poor, once he became rich.

Celebrity changes everything, yes, but not like being an unwed mother changes everything. Being a celebrity makes you publicly absurd. It makes you another Brand X on a shelf overflowing with commodities packaged and sold by money-grubbing corporations.

It's like a prominent libertarian using the oxymoron "billionaire philanthropist" to describe [journalist] Glenn Greenwald's sugar daddy Pierre Omidyar, and then calling on libertarians everywhere to implore their congressional representatives (like Rand Paul?) to pave the way for ex-pat Greenwald's safe return from self-imposed exile. Forget the 11 million undocumented aliens in the country (which libertarians are doing their best to deport), trying to stay here for a chance to work and exist in noble anonymity; you must expend your time and energy on one celeb who, single-handedly, is going to make "us" understand "what kind of country we're turning into."

Give me a break. Celebrity-making in the hands of venture capitalists and social-service wrecking libertarians renders Greenwald absurd—like he made himself absurd for taking Omidyar's blood money; like celebrity-seeking made devout Maherist-Lenoist Jeremy Scahill[1] absurd; like it makes every other denizen of late-night comedy shows, hosted by millionaire racists, in a word, absurd.

Money and Fans

In this spirit, Russell Brand has reached new heights of absurdity by predicting a coming revolution. The poster of him

---

1. Jeremy Scahill is a journalist and author. Bill Maher and Jay Leno host talk shows.

looking like Che has done more damage to his brain than all the dope he pumped into his veins; but his adoring fans believe his rubbish and, for 24 hours, happily imagine themselves as revolutionaries.

They do, after all, identify with him, and his brand of consumer absurdity. And in modern America, money and an adoring fan base are what matter.

From down here in the trenches, I wonder what Russell's brand of revolution looks like? A civil war, perhaps, in America, with well-armed Tea Partiers [a conservative Republican faction], surrendering by the score? Or will it be a worldwide uprising of the lower classes against their corporate oppressors? (Didn't someone already suggest that?) Will Brand's revolution involve people killing and being killed, or simply pretending they have the courage of their convictions, assuming they have any convictions (or critical thoughts) at all?

In any case, the powers that be are thanking Russell Brand X for reducing the on-going struggle for freedom and justice, once again, to the absurd.

> *"If celebrities are fully informed and engaged with the cause they are promoting, the message can greatly influence the process of persuading others to support the cause."*

The Thirty Most Generous Celebrities

Anderson Antunes

Anderson Antunes is a Forbes contributor. In the following viewpoint, he reports on the celebrities who gave the most to charity in 2010. The list is compiled by the Giving Back Fund in hopes of encouraging other celebrity giving. Antunes reports that while some experts are skeptical as to whether celebrity endorsement of charities increases giving, others state that celebrity association with a charity can have major effects on donations. He also says that celebrities like to be associated with charities, and charities like to be associated with celebrities; it is beneficial publicity for both parties.

As you read, consider the following questions:

1. How did the Giving Back Fund compile the list of the thirty most generous celebrities, according to Antunes?

2. According to the viewpoint, who is Christopher Reeve, and what cause did he successfully support?

3. Who was the fourth most generous celebrity according to the list, and what causes did he support?

Thanks to a record donation of $10,569,002 to the Ressler Gertz Foundation, actress Jami Gertz and her husband, Antony Ressler, top the list of the 30 Most Generous Celebrities compiled by the Giving Back Fund, a nonprofit organization that tracks philanthropic giving worldwide. Although not exactly a mainstream actress, Gertz's deep-pocketed donation has much to do with the fact that Ressler is the cofounder of Ares Capital, a Los Angeles investment firm that controls more than $40 billion in assets, which has also recently expressed interest in buying the Dodgers.

Encouragement by Example

Coming in second was musician Herb Alpert, who gave $9,104,829 to the Herb Alpert Foundation, which focuses on the arts, compassion and well-being, followed by Mel Gibson, who signed a check of $6,853,020 to the A.P. Reilly Foundation, which he started to support the Church of the Holy Family.

Authors, actors, artists, comedians, and supermodels were among the celebrities who made this year's list, which takes into account the largest donations to charity made by them in 2010, according to public records and interviews with charities known for their celebrity affiliations. The data was also compiled by interviewing publicists, attorneys, agents, agencies, and managers for information about their clients. (Donations made by a celebrity's foundation were not included on the list, since there's no way to track the source of that money, which could be money raised by the public and not necessarily donated by the celebrity.)

"Encouragement by example is the main reason we compile this list," said Marc Pollick, president and founder of the Giving Back Fund. "One cannot help but be influenced by the generosity of his or her peers," Pollick continued. "We are also often asked by the media and the public about which celebrities actually give the largest donations to charitable causes, so we decided it made sense to publish the research for all to see."

It's no surprise that celebrities like to have their names associated with good causes. It's good PR [public relations], and the more good they do, the more the public loves them. Because of that, they have often been accused of using charity work only to improve their "brand." Truth be told, charities also rely on celebrities to get press and help raise awareness. In other words, it is a virtuous (vicious?) cycle.

The question is—does it work both ways?

Do Celebrities Help?

"Never say never but, in my experience, the fabled benefits of celebrity support have rarely lived up to the hype," says Peter Stanford, a British journalist who's on the board of several charities in the UK [United Kingdom]. "I have lost count of the number of charity chief executives and chairs who've told me that they pinned their hopes on a bumper payback because they had a famous face at a fund-raising event, or fronting a campaign, and then been disappointed."

Justin Forsyth, the CEO [chief executive officer] of Save the Children, believes otherwise. "In my experience, the benefits of celebrity are not fabled but real—and can produce very concrete results. Without the campaigning energies of [singer] Bono, [singer] Bob Geldof and [actor] Richard Curtis, for example, I don't believe 46 million more children would be in school today in some of the world's poorest countries," Forsyth countered, remembering the success of the Make Poverty History and Drop the Debt campaigns.

The book *Exploring Public Relations,* written by public relations and communications experts Ralph Tench and Liz Yeomans, attributes the effectiveness of celebrity endorsement to 'credibility' and 'attention.' The authors go on to say that celebrities can attract attention and this is the most vital ingredient of success in a world saturated with so much noise generated by media messages. If celebrities are fully informed and engaged with the cause they are promoting, the message can greatly influence the process of persuading others to support the cause.

An example of that premise is the collaboration between the late actor Christopher Reeve and the American Paralysis Association (APA). After Reeve was paralyzed in a horse-riding accident in 1995 he became connected with the APA, which over the next three years saw its revenue double to $5 million, according to the *Chronicle of Philanthropy.* In fact, the results were so positive that the charity was rebranded as the Christopher Reeve Foundation [and later the Christopher & Dana Reeve Foundation].

[Cyclist] Lance Armstrong has had a similar impact on cancer awareness. The famous US cyclist, a seven-time Tour de France champion and a survivor of testicular cancer, is the founder of the Livestrong anti-cancer foundation, which annually helps millions of sick people, although critics have leveled charges against it for spending much of its budget on buffing Armstrong's personal brand. Besides the financial support of its founder, the foundation also raises funds through licensing arrangements with companies like Nike, Bayer and Oakley. Today, Livestrong has a yearly revenue of around $48 million.[1]

Combined, the 30 most generous celebrities donated nearly $64 million of their personal wealth to a variety of charities.

---

1. Livestrong disconnected with Armstrong in late 2012 after his admission of performance-enhancing drug use.

Either for doing the good deed or simply for other reasons, these people certainly cannot be accused of not giving back.

The List

Check out who made the 30 Most Generous Celebrities list:

1. Actress Jami Gertz and her husband, Antony Ressler—$10,569,002

To the Ressler Gertz Foundation. Grants from the foundation include $1.7 million to the LA [Los Angeles] County Museum of Art, $400k to Cedars-Sinai Medical Center.

2. Musician Herb Alpert—$9,104,829

To the Herb Alpert Foundation, which focuses on the arts, compassion, and well-being.

3. Actor Mel Gibson—$6,853,020

To the A.P. Reilly Foundation, which he started to support the Church of the Holy Family.

4. Director, Producer, Writer, George Lucas—$4,250,000

To Lucasfilm Foundation then granted to the George Lucas Educational Foundation with a mission to inspire and empower young people to become responsible citizens, compassionate leaders, and to live their dream.

5. Writer Nora Roberts—$3,000,000

To the Nora Roberts Foundation, which supports literacy. Additional areas of focus are children's programs, arts organizations, and humanitarian efforts, with local organizations being its priority.

6. NFL [National Football League] player Ndamukong Suh—$2,600,000

$2 million to the Nebraska University athletic department and another $600,000 to the University of Nebraska–Lincoln College of Engineering to endow a scholarship. It is the largest single gift ever from a former football player.

7. MLB [Major League Baseball] player Lance Berkman and his wife, Cara—$2,412,245

To the Lord's Fund, a foundation they established. Grants include $400k to Josiah Venture, a Christian youth movement in Eastern Europe, and $113k to Children's Cup, a Christian organization focusing on "forgotten children" in Swaziland, Mozambique and Zimbabwe, and efforts are also under way in Vietnam and the Philippines. Most of their giving is to Christian-based organizations.

8. Actress Meryl Streep and her husband, Donald Gummer—$2,000,000

To Silver Mountain Foundation for the Arts, a foundation they established. Grants include $100k each to Oxfam America and Partners in Health; $1,225,000 to Vassar College. Total grant making for the year was more than $2.1 million.

9. Television producer Marcy Carsey and her husband, John Carsey—$1,870,000

To Carsey Family Foundation they established. Grants include $250k to Media Matters for America, $100k to Institute for America's Future, $50k to Progressive Talent Initiative.

10. *The Simpsons* co-creator Sam Simon—$1,800,000

To the Sam Simon Foundation to "save the lives of dogs to enrich the lives of people." The foundation manages a number of programs including a mobile veterinary unit, dogs for veterans, and dogs for people who are deaf or hard of hearing.

11. Comedian Jerry Seinfeld—$1,766,000

To the Seinfeld Family Foundation that supports education, children's services, health associations, and Jewish organizations; funding also for the arts.

12. Actress Barbra Streisand—$1,555,500

To the Streisand Foundation. Grants are distributed to a variety of charities and causes including the Barbra Streisand Women's Cardiovascular Research and Education Program at Cedars-Sinai, City Year, and the Natural Resources Defense Council, respectively.

13. Actor Matthew McConaughey—$1,537,292

To the Just Keep Livin Foundation that he established. Grants distributed include $88,000 to Communities in Schools Los Angeles West and $38,000 Communities in Schools of Central Texas.

14. Writers Dean and Gerda Koontz—$1,500,000

To the Dean and Gerda Koontz Foundation. Grants include $750,000 to Canine Companions for Independence and $500,000 to Saint Michael's Abbey in Silverado, CA.

15. Model Gisele Bündchen—$1,500,000

To the Red Cross for Haiti Relief.

16. Writer Isabel Allende—$1,017,247

To the Isabel Allende Foundation to support charities that empower and protect women. Founded in honor of her daughter, Paula Frias, who passed away at 28. Grants include $500,000 to Oritel, which provides human services for low-income families and $30,500 to the Global Fund for Women.

17. Actor Alec Baldwin—$1,005,131

To the Alec Baldwin Foundation. Grants include $50,000 to the NY [New York] Philharmonic, $42,500 to Waterkeeper Alliance, and $250,000 to the Carol M. Baldwin Breast Cancer Research [Fund].

18. Actress Sandra Bullock—$1,000,000

To Doctors Without Borders for Haiti relief following the devastating earthquake.

19. NFL player Eli Manning and his wife, Abby—$1,000,000

To the University of Mississippi's Ole Miss Opportunity [Program], which allows prospective students with an adjusted gross family income at or below $30,000 to attend the University of Mississippi.

20. Actors Will and Jada Smith—$900,000

To the Will and Jada Smith Family Foundation. Grants included $126,000 to the Lupus Foundation [of America], $200,000 to the Baltimore School for the Arts, and $52,000 to the Make-A-Wish Foundation.

21. *Playboy* founder Hugh Hefner—$900,000

To the Trust for Public Land to save the iconic Hollywood sign from being plowed under in order to make room for four luxury homes.

22. NBA [National Basketball Association] player Carmelo Anthony—$837,200

To Carmelo Anthony Foundation. Grants include $500,000 to Syracuse University and $302,000 to the Living Classrooms Foundation.

23. Cyclist and seven-time winner of the Tour de France, Lance Armstrong—$700,648

To the Livestrong Foundation, which he founded to improve the lives of people with cancer.

24. Writers Jonathan and Faye Kellerman—$627,700

To Jonathan and Faye Kellerman Foundation. Grants include $175,000 for Children's Hospital [Los Angeles], $150,000 to USC [University of Southern California]/Kellerman endowment, $25,000 to Boston Institute of Music.

25. MLB player Mariano Rivera—$627,500

To the Mariano Rivera Foundation. Grants distributed included $150,000 to the Church of God Prophecy and $50,000 to the Brooklyn Tabernacle.

26. Singer/songwriter Taylor Swift—$625,000

$500k to Hands on Nashville, the Community Foundation of Middle Tennessee for Nashville's flood relief efforts (Nashville Rising); $25,000 to the Wyomissing, PA, school district for education; $100,000 check to rebuild Kids Kingdom, a playground in Hendersonville, Tennessee, where she attended high school.

27. Daniel and Cara Whitney (Larry the Cable Guy)— $550,020

To Git-R-Done Foundation. Grants include $500,000 to the Child Advocacy Center and $525,000 to the Madonna Foundation.

28. Artist Jasper Johns—$500,000

To Low Road Foundation, which he established. Grants distributed include $50,000 to the Foundation for Contemporary Arts.

29. Golfer Davis Love—$424,379

To the Davis Love Foundation, which he established. Grants distributed include $479,000 to the St. [Simons] Presbyterian Church, $100,000 to Frederica Academy, $75,000 to Special Olympics, and $75,000 to Boys and Girls Club of Southeast GA.

30. Actress Victoria Principal—$342,665

To Victoria Principal Foundation. Grants distributed include $25,000 to Greenpeace Fund, $125,000 to Natural Resources Defense Council, $100,000 to Oceana.

| "It's easy to see why news outlets and do-gooder celebrities flocked to [Somaly] Mam's cause. The American media worry about no one as much as . . . young women, in particular their sexual exploitation."

Celebrity Philanthropy May Be Misguided and Misleading

Kat Stoeffel

Kat Stoeffel is a writer for New York *magazine. In the following viewpoint, she discusses the story of Somaly Mam, a Cambodian activist who works against sex trafficking and who has said she was sold into sex slavery herself at an early age. Many celebrities, including journalist Nicholas Kristof, found Mam's story compelling and promoted her charity. However, it was eventually reported that much of Mam's story was fabricated and that she routinely lied to donors and encouraged other women she worked with to lie about their backgrounds. Stoeffel concludes that celebrity activists such as Mam can end up miring their causes in scandal.*

As you read, consider the following questions:

1. Besides AnnaLynne McCord, what other celebrities were drawn to Mam's cause, according to Stoeffel?

2. What parts of Mam's story does Stoeffel say have been called into question?

3. How did Meas Ratha's real story differ from the story she initially told the press, and why does Stoeffel say the difference is important?

Before actress AnnaLynne McCord was ready to share the story of her sexual assault in the pages [of] *Cosmopolitan*, she found solace in the work of Cambodian anti-sex-trafficking campaigner Somaly Mam. McCord visited the shelters Mam built for girls who escaped the sex trade—as Mam herself did—and met "dozens" of young survivors who had been "kidnapped or sold" into sex slavery "as young as four or five," then rescued from "grimy brothels where they are raped every day." "Through helping them heal," McCord told the magazine, "I began to heal myself." Now she visits Cambodia every year.

Fabricated Stories

McCord was far from the only celebrity drawn in by Mam's feel-good mission and personal magnetism. [Actress] Susan Sarandon's trip to the rehab shelters for girls rescued in Mam's brothel raids was documented by *Condé Nast Traveler*. [Actress] Meg Ryan joined *New York Times* reporter Nicholas Kristof in Cambodia to visit Mam's shelters for his PBS documentary *Half the Sky*. Tech PR [public relations] guru Brandee Barker joined the board of the Somaly Mam Foundation, of which [technology executive] Sheryl Sandberg is an advisory member. Yet despite raising millions of dollars (and receiving accolades from the State Department and the U.N. [United Nations]), Mam's story has turned out to be a cautionary tale about the risks of celebrity philanthropy.

Last week, a *Newsweek* cover story revealed that Mam had been publicizing her efforts with fabricated, lurid stories about herself and the girls in her shelters, which sex trafficking experts say dangerously misconstrued the problem at hand. In her autobiography, *The Road of Lost Innocence*, Mam wrote that an abusive grandfather figure sold her virginity when she was 14, after which she spent a decade in a brothel. But Mam's Cambodian friends and neighbors denied the existence of the grandfather figure to *Newsweek*, and say she finished high school. Another girl, Long Pross, told [talk show host] Oprah Winfrey and Kristof that she had been kidnapped, tortured with electric wires, and had an eye gouged out by an angry pimp before Mam rescued her. *Newsweek* found medical records saying Pross had surgery at age 13 to remove a non-malignant tumor. The hospital referred her to Mam's organization, AFESIP, "to see if they could admit Pross to one of their vocational training programs." Mam resigned from the foundation named for her late last week, following a probe by an outside law firm (though she stands by her autobiography, according to Kristof).

It's easy to see why news outlets and do-gooder celebrities flocked to Mam's cause. The American media worry about no one as much as they do young women, in particular their sexual exploitation. The younger, the more fuel for our outrage. (Never mind that experts told *Newsweek* it is rare to unheard of to see prepubescent children in brothels, as Mam and McCord claimed.) Mam brought to the cause the credibility of a survivor—however dubious—plus telegenic good looks to rival her celebrity advocates. It seemed like a perfect package.

Celebrity for Reporter

But another problem was that Mam's tied-up-in-a-bow cause made a celebrity out of a journalist: Her loudest champion by far was *New York Times* columnist Nicholas Kristof, who devoted numerous columns to Mam's work, treating the

Sex Work and Economics

"The twin assumptions that no woman would willingly sell sex and that sex workers lack education and skills for 'decent' work are central to the issues playing out in Cambodia," writes Cheryl Overs, author of the 2009 AP-NSW [Asia Pacific Network of Sex Workers] report "Caught Between the Tiger and the Crocodile: The Campaign to Suppress Human Trafficking and Sexual Exploitation in Cambodia." In truth, many have also worked in garment factories, and left the factories due to low wages to move into sex work. The APNSW logo, a sewing machine with a red circle and slash through it, is a nod to all of this. Although anti-prostitution NGOs [nongovernmental organizations] such as International Justice Mission and AFESIP . . . claim to teach women they have "rescued" and "recovered" from brothels to operate sewing machines at their Cambodian shelters, sex and garment workers together call attention to the poor conditions in the factories that make sex work a higher-paying, more attractive alternative.

Melissa Gira Grant, Playing the Whore: The Work of Sex Work. *New York: Verso, 2014.*

made-up Long Pross story as gospel in a column and his docu-series. As Kristof inserted himself into his reporting, he became something of a humanitarian-celebrity himself, purchasing the freedom of two Cambodian sex workers and live-tweeting a brothel raid. In a short blog post, Kristof now says he is hesitant to be the arbiter of Mam's biography (a little late for that), and urges readers not to let one woman's backstory "overtake the imperative of ending the trafficking of young teenagers into brothels." That wasn't nearly good enough for the *New York Times'* public editor Margaret Sullivan, who said Kristof "owes it to his readers to explain, to the best of his ability and at length, what happened and why."

To a certain extent, I sympathize with Kristof. It feels strange to nitpick the origin myth of someone so committed to such an obviously worthy cause. According to *Newsweek*, another girl Mam claimed to have saved from child prostitution, Meas Ratha, later confessed to fabricating and rehearsing the story she gave French television crews (and even auditioning for the role), in the service of the cause. "Somaly said that . . . if I want to help another woman I have to do [the interview] very well," she told *Newsweek*. But if Kristof had done his journalistic nitpicking duty, we would have learned that Meas Ratha, like Long Pross, came to Mam not to escape an evil pimp, but out of much less lurid economic desperation. (Her family couldn't afford to raise her and her six siblings.) That's the larger problem behind sex slavery, according to *Playing the Whore[: The Work of Sex Work]* author Melissa Gira Grant, as well as the much more commonly trafficked domestic, garment, and agricultural workers. "Ending abuse in the sex trade requires action that is less telegenic than a photo op or a gala," Grant explained in a Friday op-ed column. "It's a broader fight against poverty, inequality and vulnerability that goes far beyond a brothel's walls."

> *"We need a system that does not create so many billionaires and, until we do that, this kind of philanthropy is either a distraction or potentially harmful to the need for systemic change to the political economy."*

The Flip Side to Bill Gates' Charity Billions

Andrew Bowman

Andrew Bowman is a journalist for New Internationalist *magazine. In the following viewpoint, he argues that the massive philanthropic giving of billionaires such as Bill Gates has potential downsides. Gates is donating so much money that he can set the world health agenda in many ways, Bowman says, but Gates is not accountable to any democratic institutions. As a result, Gates may pursue policies that are not necessarily the priorities of people in donor countries. For example, Gates has worked to protect drug patents, though loosening them might ultimately be the best way to get medicine to third world countries. Ultimately, Bowman concludes, a system that creates enormous divides be-*

tween rich and poor is itself the problem, and philanthropy by the very rich does not address that issue, and may even exacerbate it.

As you read, consider the following questions:

1. According to the viewpoint, how much money did the Gates Foundation give in grants in 2010?
2. On what game-changing health technologies does the Gates Foundation focus, according to Bowman?
3. What issue does Bowman say will test the mettle of the Gates Foundation?

Microsoft's former CEO has made record-breaking donations to global health programmes—but an investigation by Andrew Bowman reveals some unpleasant side effects.

Last year, Bill Gates reminisced in the *Huffington Post* about his first trip to Africa in 1993. 'I saw that many of the world's lifesaving, life-enhancing discoveries were not available in Africa,' he said. 'That was deeply upsetting. . . . I became convinced that if science and technology were better applied to the challenges of Africa, the tremendous potential of the continent would be unleashed and people could be healthier and fulfil their promise.' Having spent 18 years making as much money as possible with Microsoft (the computer software company he cofounded in 1975), in 1994 Gates started giving it away.

Philanthropic funds are common among the super-rich in the US; they enable tax avoidance provided five per cent of net investment assets are given away annually. What quickly set Gates' fund apart was its orientation towards the poor— rather than elite culture or religion—and its sheer size.

Targeting global health and US education, Gates' giving rapidly ballooned into the billions. In 2006, his friend Warren Buffett (the business magnate currently ranked the world's third richest person) pledged $31 billion in company stock to the Bill and Melinda Gates Foundation. Combined with Gates' committed assets of over $30 billion, this made it arguably the biggest philanthropic venture ever. That year, its Global Development Program extended its activities to agriculture and economic development and, with projects multiplying, Gates began working full time on philanthropy in 2008.

In 2010, the foundation gave $2.5 billion in grants—80 per cent to international projects. In total it has disbursed over $26 billion, most of it to global health. To put these figures into perspective: since 1914 the Rockefeller Foundation has given $14 billion (adjusted to today's values). Only the US and British governments give more to global health today. The World Health Organization (WHO), meanwhile, operates on less than $2 billion a year.

The foundation's achievements are undoubtedly impressive. Through supporting vaccination programmes, for example, it claims to have saved nearly six million lives. With rich world enthusiasm for foreign aid wavering, on 26 January this year Gates committed a further $750 million to the Global Fund to Fight AIDS, Tuberculosis and Malaria—an organization he claims saves 100,000 lives a month. Admirers credit the foundation with putting global health back on world leaders' agendas and, through Gates' Giving Pledge initiative, encouraging several other US multibillionaires to pledge their wealth to charity. What's not to like?

Accountable to Whom?

Philanthropy—and particularly philanthropy on this scale—isn't a black-and-white issue though, and important questions have been raised about the way the foundation operates, and the impact of its work.

The first question concerns accountability. While only around five per cent of the foundation's annual global health funding goes directly to lobbying and advocacy, this money (over $100 million) talks loudly. Gates funds institutions ranging from US university departments to major international development NGOs. The foundation is the main player in several global health partnerships and one of the single largest donors to the WHO. This gives it considerable leverage in shaping health policy priorities and intellectual norms.

Gregg Gonsalves, an experienced AIDS activist and cofounder of the International Treatment Preparedness Coalition, welcomes the foundation's funding, but is concerned about its power. 'Depending on what side of bed Gates gets out of in the morning,' he remarks, 'it can shift the terrain of global health.'

The foundation's 26 strategies are reviewed annually, and although CEO Jeff Raikes stresses that it is making 'a systematic effort to listen' to grantees, Gonsalves and others are sceptical: 'It's not a democracy. It's not even a constitutional monarchy. It's about what Bill and Melinda want. We depend on them learning, and it's not as if there are many points of influence for this.'

'The foundation is more than a collection of grants and projects,' says Dr David McCoy, a public health doctor and researcher at University College London and an advisor to the People's Health Movement. 'Through its funding it also operates through an interconnected network of organizations and individuals across academia and the NGO and business sectors. This allows it to leverage influence through a kind of "group-think" in international health.' In 2008 the WHO's head of malaria research, Arata Kochi, accused a Gates Foundation 'cartel' of suppressing diversity of scientific opinion, claiming the organization was 'accountable to no-one other than itself'.

Seeking Miracles

In what direction, then, has the foundation been pushing global health policy? Warren Buffett once said of his approach to finance: 'I don't look to jump over seven-foot bars. I look around for one-foot bars I can step over.' Gates asserts his philosophy of philanthropy to be the opposite: 'We should be looking around for the seven-foot bars; that's why we exist.'

This entails game-changing technologies, specifically vaccines—'a miracle because with three doses you can prevent deadly diseases for an entire lifetime'. Just as a vaccine eliminated smallpox in the 20th century, science could, Gates hopes, do the same for AIDS, malaria and tuberculosis in the 21st. Research on new drugs and vaccines has been the single largest destination for his funds, receiving 36.5 per cent of grants given between 1998 and 2007.

Through the public-private GAVI Alliance—which Gates helped found a decade ago with an initial grant of $750 million and which aims to increase access to immunization—vaccines for Hepatitis B and the Hib bacteria have been brought into widespread use. GAVI's current focus is on new vaccines for pneumococcus and rotavirus—causes of pneumonia and diarrhoea—which could, it suggests, save nearly 700,000 lives by 2015.

Making Greed Good?

Coupled with a belief in science and innovation is Gates' vision of 'creative capitalism'. Setting out his approach at the 2008 World Economic Forum in Davos, he said: 'There are two great forces: self-interest and caring for others.' To reconcile the two, the foundation pursues partnerships in which, guided by NGOs, academics and assorted 'stakeholders', donor funds are used to overcome the 'market failures' which deny the poor access to medicine, by paying pharmaceutical companies to sell their products cheaper and pursue research projects they would otherwise ignore.

Through GAVI, the foundation claims to have lowered the costs of Hepatitis B inoculations by 68 per cent, and is supporting a $1.5 billion 'advanced market commitment' to develop pneumococcal vaccines.

For supporters, it's a win-win: the poor get new medicines faster and cheaper; and, as the *Financial Times* explains, it's a leg up for pharmaceutical companies 'seeking to expand into faster-growing, lower-income countries where they need to charge less and co-operate more' to share the risks of development.

The arrangements have, however, created concerns. As Tido von Schoen-Angerer, executive director of the Access Campaign at Médecins Sans Frontierès, explains, 'The foundation wants the private sector to do more on global health, and sets up partnerships with the private sector involved in governance. As these institutions are clearly also trying to influence policy making, there are huge conflicts of interests . . . the companies should not play a role in setting the rules of the game.'

The Gates Foundation is one of the single largest donors to the World Health Organization. This gives it considerable leverage in shaping health policy priorities.

The foundation itself has employed numerous former Big Pharma figures, leading to accusations of industry bias. Many campaigners see loosening intellectual property laws as a better way of increasing access to medicines, both in lowering prices through generic competition and in enabling innovation outside patent-hoarding companies.

However, Microsoft lobbied vociferously for the World Trade Organization's TRIPS agreement (the agreement on trade-related aspects of intellectual property), which obliges member countries to defend patents for a minimum of 20 years after the filing date. As recently as 2007, Microsoft was lobbying the G8 to tighten global intellectual property (IP) protection, a move that would, Oxfam said, 'worsen the health crisis in developing countries'.

Global access agreements—to keep prices low and share results—are required for companies receiving foundation money, von Schoen-Angerer says, 'but could they go further? Definitely yes. In examples like GAVI, industry gets quite beneficial deals.' Gonsalves, himself HIV positive, explains, 'I would be dead were it not for the pharmaceutical industry. That said, a lot more people will be dead if we don't have robust generic competition.'

The Gates' mettle will be tested around the combustible issue of IP in middle-income countries. Big Pharma is sometimes willing to relax IP for the world's poorest nations, but rarely in emerging markets—which still contain most of the world's poorest people.

Philanthrocapitalism vs. Democracy?

Gates' philanthropy seeks not just to make businesses more charitable, but to make charity more businesslike. Dubbed 'philanthrocapitalism' or 'venture philanthropy', the approach is based on NGOs competing for grants with their performance evaluated using business metrics.

According to Gates, 'our net effect should be to save years of life for well under $100; so, if we waste even $500,000, we are wasting 5,000 years of life.' Under these terms, the best results are achieved through 'vertically' funded projects—interventions targeted at specific diseases or health problems, largely bypassing existing health systems. The payoffs from 'horizontal' integration with public-health systems can, in contrast, be comparatively slow to materialize and hard to measure.

A study in the *Lancet* in 2009 showed only 1.4 per cent of the foundation's grants between 1998 and 2007 went to public-sector organizations, while of the 659 NGOs receiving grants, only 37 were headquartered in low- or middle-income countries.

In many majority world countries, state health care was eviscerated by structural adjustment programmes enforced by the World Bank and International Monetary Fund, and by the continued loss of skilled personnel in globalized labour markets. Now, says McCoy, NGOs have stepped into the breach but have also created a 'fragmented "patchwork quilt" landscape of healthcare provision' which governments struggle to coordinate and align to national priorities.

This has potentially serious implications. Polly Clayden of i-Base, an HIV information and activist organization, says, 'some of the research Gates funds is ill-advised, but if you had HIV and somebody was paying for your antiretroviral drugs in a trial, perhaps you wouldn't really care [who provided it]. What you really want is for those people to be treated.'

'However,' she warns, 'the problem is sustainability. Donors are quite capricious: AIDS might be the priority one year, and then suddenly they will go on to something else.'

Research by Devi Sridhar at Oxford University warns that philanthropic interventions are 'radically skewing public health programmes towards issues of the greatest concern to wealthy donors'. 'Issues,' she writes, 'which are not necessarily top priority for people in the recipient country.'

The situation is replicated at an international level. With the rise of health partnerships, the proportion of global health funding channeled through the UN fell from 32 to 14 per cent between 1990 and 2008, placing major limits on the possibility for poorer nations to influence international health policy. Although the Gates Foundation provides considerable support to the WHO, the money is, as with much of the WHO's funding nowadays, earmarked for preconceived projects rather than the decisions of the World Health Assembly.

For critics, then, the way 'venture philanthropy' focuses on measurable impact may obscure the less tangible, but equally important, goals of democracy and empowerment. As the philanthropy analyst Michael Edwards has asked: 'Would philanthrocapitalism have helped fund the civil rights movement in the US? I hope so, but it wasn't "data driven", it didn't operate through competition, it couldn't generate much revenue, and it didn't measure its impact in terms of the numbers of people who were served each day. Yet it changed the world forever.'

The Fruit or the Trees?

Mark Harrington, director of the Treatment Action Group, an AIDS advocacy think tank which has received foundation money in the past, also feels that, ultimately, democratically accountable governments should solve global health problems, but that in the absence of their commitment there is a need for pragmatism.

'Medical research and global health are both public goods: the benefits accrue to everyone, even though only some people pay for them. Industry will only do it if they see return on investment; and philanthropists, well, it's better Gates doing this with his money than what the Koch brothers [funders of the right-wing Tea Party political movement in the US] are doing with theirs. Do I think it's good that we live in a world where some people have so much money? Not really, but I don't get to choose that. We have to work with the world the way it is.'

McCoy insists, however, that it is important to mount a challenge: 'Appealing to the mega-rich to be more charitable is not a solution to global health problems. We need a system that does not create so many billionaires and, until we do that, this kind of philanthropy is either a distraction or potentially harmful to the need for systemic change to the political economy.'

Carlos Slim, the Mexican multibillionaire who replaced Gates at the top of the world's rich list (due to Gates' charity), likened philanthropy to owning an orchard: 'You have to give away the fruit, but not the trees.' He and Gates are products of an economic system that has produced monopolies and redistributed wealth upwards for 30 years. Parallels may be drawn between the inequalities of today and the Victorian era, when health provision for the poor depended on the largesse of the rich. Oscar Wilde observed of the philanthropists of that era: 'They seriously and very sentimentally set themselves to the task of remedying the evils that they see in poverty, but their remedies do not cure the disease: they merely prolong it.' Then and now, as Wilde said, 'the proper aim is to try and reconstruct society on such a basis that poverty will be impossible.'

Periodical and Internet Sources Bibliography

The following articles have been selected to supplement the diverse views presented in this chapter.

Alcibiades Bilzerian	"Hypocrisy in Philanthropy?," *Bilzerian Report*, February 8, 2012.
Evelyn Burnett and Nadia Owusu	"One Shoe: Why Celebrity Philanthropy Needs to Think Bigger," Living Cities, September 5, 2012.
Sandy Cohen	"Celebrity Charity Galas: Are They Any Good for Non-Profits?," *Huffington Post*, October 18, 2012.
John Colapinto	"Looking Good: The New Boom in Celebrity Philanthropy," *New Yorker*, March 26, 2012.
Paula Froelich	"Which Celebrity Charities Should You Trust with Your Donations?," Fox News, June 12, 2012.
Paula Lavigne	"Athlete Charities Often Lack Standards," ESPN, March 31, 2013.
Alexis Okeowo	"Celebrity and Charity in Africa," *New Yorker*, December 18, 2013.
Martha Petrocheilos	"Celebrity Culture and Charity," *Beaver Online* (London), February 6, 2014.
Cliff Prior	"Social Enterprise Celebrities: The Good and the Bad," *Guardian*, November 29, 2013.
Alice Robb	"America: Celebrities Can Make a Real-World Difference, but Few Do (Chart)," *New Republic*, November 6, 2013.
Guy Sorman	"The Philanthropic Spectacle," *City Journal*, Autumn 2013.

CHAPTER 3

How Does Celebrity Culture Affect Particular Groups?

Chapter Preface

In 2009 singer Chris Brown was arrested and charged for battery of his then girlfriend, singer Rihanna. Photos of Rihanna with visible injuries were leaked to the press, and there was a media firestorm. Brown and Rihanna later reconciled, and in 2013 had begun dating again, which once more created a wave of public concern.

Many commentators have written about the implications of this incident and its media coverage for victims of domestic violence. Ben Sisario in an April 28, 2013, article in the *New York Times* quoted University of Pennsylvania professor Salamishah Tillet as stating, "This is the case that has defined dating and domestic violence for the hip-hop generation." Some sites, including HollywoodLife.com, were enthusiastic about the reunion; editor Bonnie Fuller said that after consulting with experts she believed that "there are definitely men who can turn their lives around." Laurel Eisner, former executive director of domestic violence help group Sanctuary for Families, disagreed, saying that HollywoodLife.com was sending a dangerous and false message to young girls. "There is almost nothing to support the notion that a man who is as impulsive and as close to anger as he [Chris Brown] is, and who continues to repeat misogynist messages—there isn't any evidence that men like that will change."

Natasha Patterson and Camilla A. Sears in a spring 2011 article in the journal *Genders* argued that the media framing around the incident tended to focus on Rihanna rather than on Chris Brown. Rihanna is presented in media narratives as "a 'can-do' girl who takes responsibility for the abuse by monitoring her actions and being careful not to be viewed or framed as a victim. In such a way, Chris Brown is 'let off the hook' because he experiences few negative consequences for his actions."

Phoebe Eccles in an August 23, 2012, essay at *Feminspire* said that judging Rihanna was unhelpful and counterproductive. She pointed out that in Boston, a poll showed that 50 percent of teens blamed Rihanna for the assault, while many commenters expected Rihanna "to set an example" and criticized her for reconciling with Brown. Eccles concluded that "at the end of the day, we place too much value on celebrity culture. Rihanna does not owe us anything. . . . *Society should be helping people in Rihanna's situation, instead of expecting them to know what to do."*

Eccles further added, "In the meanwhile, we must be aware that the lives of celebrities cannot be leaned on too heavily when searching for guidance in how to deal with domestic violence." Rihanna should not be blamed for her actions, she said, but neither should she be seen as a model for others in dealing with domestic violence.

The following chapter debates how particular groups, such as children, women, and members of the gay and lesbian community, are affected by celebrity culture.

"Once seen as a defiant and courageous act . . . coming out has lost some of its potency."

Coming Out: When Love Dares Speak, and Nobody Listens

Jeremy W. Peters

Jeremy W. Peters is a reporter in the Washington bureau of the New York Times. In the following viewpoint, he writes that in the past when celebrities came out as gay it generated much media and public interest, including both praise and hostility. Now, however, he argues, lesbian, gay, and bisexual individuals are more accepted, and when celebrities come out it is often seen as routine. He notes also that many people feel that celebrities come out to generate attention or promote their work, and so the public is less impressed than they might have been in the past. He says, though, that when stars from conservative communities come out it can still have an impact.

As you read, consider the following questions:

1. What does Eric Marcus say is more important in changing people's attitudes toward gay individuals than celebrities coming out?

2. According to Howard Bragman, why is it significant that Chely Wright and Ricky Martin came out?

3. Under what circumstances does Peters say that coming out can still get a lot of attention?

The love that dare not speak its name has been speaking up an awful lot lately. So much, in fact, that people are starting not to notice when it happens.

Coming Out Has Become Commonplace

Barely five months into the year, several high-profile people have come out, from [singer] Ricky Martin, to the [TV show] *Will and Grace* star Sean Hayes, to the country music singer Chely Wright. Yet Americans greeted the news largely with a shrug.

In Mr. Martin's case, the most common reaction in the United States was hardly surprise. Ditto for Mr. Hayes, who played the flighty, foppish Jack McFarland on the hit NBC series and who is now on Broadway in *Promises, Promises*. (More on that later.) For Ms. Wright, who was little known outside of her country music fan base until she came out, the response was most often, "Who?"

Once seen as a defiant and courageous act of such social and political significance that gay rights activists created a holiday for it and recruited prominent gay people to take part (National Coming Out Day, still observed every Oct. 11), coming out has lost some of its potency.

While few experts on gay issues would dispute the powerful impact that coming out has on a personal, one-on-one level, there is a growing sense that a celebrity coming out sways few hearts and minds and does relatively little to alter negative perceptions about gay people.

"There's the assumption among gay people that if only this famous person came out, things would be better—and that's never been the case," said Eric Marcus, a chronicler of gay social issues, whose books on the subject include *Making History: The Struggle for Gay and Lesbian Equal Rights, 1945– 1990.*

"The most significant effort any of us can make in moving the ball forward in terms of promoting awareness and acceptance of this issue is for those of us who are gay to come out to those closest to us," he said. "It isn't ultimately the celebrity that changes people's minds, or the politician. It's the individual, one on one."

The Gay and Lesbian Alliance Against Defamation [GLAAD] conducted a survey in late 2008 that looked at the reasons behind society's evolving tolerance for gay people. It found that the reason cited most frequently by people who reported having more favorable views—by far—was knowing someone who is gay.

Seventy-nine percent of the survey's respondents said that knowing someone who is gay contributed to their more positive opinions, compared with 34 percent who said seeing gay characters on television was a factor.

Ellen DeGeneres

In 1997, when [actor and comedian] Ellen DeGeneres broke ground and set out on the now familiar ritual of the celebrity coming out—a series of carefully placed magazine and television interviews that often coincide with the promotion of a product—it was a big deal.

She appeared on the cover of *Time* under the headline, "Yep, I'm Gay." The ABC studio where her show was filmed was evacuated because of a bomb threat. The Rev. Jerry Falwell mocked her as "Ellen Degenerate." At the time, with far fewer public figures comfortable with sharing their sexual orientation, Ms. DeGeneres's coming out sparked a national discussion in a way that would be surprising today.

The relative indifference Americans have these days about high-profile people coming out appears rooted not only in progressively tolerant views of gay people but also in the rather cynical supposition that stars wait to come out until they see a financial benefit, or have little to lose. Mr. Martin is past the prime of his career. Ms. Wright is promoting an album and a new book about her life as a closeted lesbian, and her revelation gives her exposure to a potential fan base outside traditional country audiences.

"With more and more gays and lesbians coming out in middle school and high school, it's hard not to view coming out post-peak in your career or whenever as cowardly, if not opportunistic," said Dan Savage, the gay author and editorial director of *The Stranger*, a Seattle newsweekly, where he writes an advice column called "Savage Love."

"Now that I have my millions, now that it's totally safe, now that I can scoop up a few more fans, I will come out," Mr. Savage added. "Forgive me, but I have much more admiration for those kids coming out in middle school."

Howard Bragman—the publicist who represents Ms. Wright and has advised other celebrities on coming out, including Meredith Baxter, the *Family Ties* actress, and Sheryl Swoopes, the pro basketball star—does not dispute that many of his clients have been motivated by profit. But he said that to confuse their desire to make money with a lack of earnestness about living openly would be unfair and a double standard.

"That doesn't make someone's coming out less sincere," he said. "Celebrities profit all the time from getting married and selling their pictures to magazines and telling their love stories in song and in book. Yeah, we'd like a little piece of the pie, too."

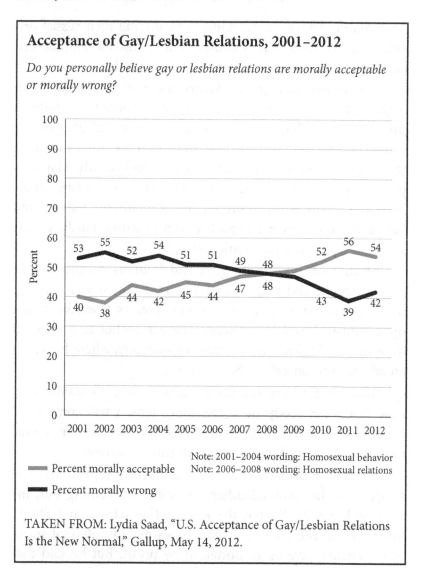

Acceptance of Gay/Lesbian Relations, 2001–2012

Do you personally believe gay or lesbian relations are morally acceptable or morally wrong?

Note: 2001–2004 wording: Homosexual behavior
Note: 2006–2008 wording: Homosexual relations

━━━ Percent morally acceptable
━━━ Percent morally wrong

TAKEN FROM: Lydia Saad, "U.S. Acceptance of Gay/Lesbian Relations Is the New Normal," Gallup, May 14, 2012.

It Can Still Matter

Mr. Bragman and others who have looked at the response to celebrities' coming out say that many people who are quick to dismiss these celebrities as opportunists fail to see the impact that they are having in the socially conservative communities they come from—in Ms. Wright's case, the country music world; and in Mr. Martin's, Latin America.

The country music star John Rich, of the duo Big & Rich, has publicly apologized for an exchange he had with Ms. Wright, recounted in her new book, in which he responded, "Good, thank God," after she denied being a lesbian.

In Puerto Rico, the archbishop of San Juan, where Mr. Martin grew up, urged compassion for the singer.

"When it's one of their own, I think it forces people to take it a little more seriously," said Jarrett Barrios, president of the Gay and Lesbian Alliance Against Defamation. "In that way, Chely Wright has the promise of being far more impactful in coming out in red states where people couldn't give two hoots about Ellen DeGeneres." The same applies to Mr. Martin in Latin America, he added, noting that the singer enjoys far greater celebrity there than he does in the United States.

But being perceived as gay can still be an issue. In an online review of *Promises, Promises*, the *Newsweek* columnist Ramin Setoodeh posited that Mr. Hayes was not a credible romantic lead in the show because of his sexual orientation. "Frankly, it's weird seeing Hayes play straight," Mr. Setoodeh wrote. "He comes off as wooden and insincere, like he's trying to hide something, which of course he is." The column sparked an immediate outcry among gay activists, and an angry response from Mr. Hayes's co-star, Kristin Chenoweth, and the magazine later tried to make amends by publishing follow-up interviews with, among others, the openly gay screenwriter (and Oscar winner for *Milk*) Dustin Lance Black.

Still, in the United States, it appears that short of a truly major celebrity or public figure unexpectedly coming out, the only surefire way one's sexuality will gain considerable attention these days is if the outing is involuntary, as was the case with Ted Haggard, the disgraced Colorado pastor, or Larry Craig, the former Idaho senator.

"Look at the cases that get attention," said Mike Rogers, who runs *BlogActive*, a [blog] that tries to force gay politicians out of the closet. "It's all salaciousness."

But that might not be bad for the advancement of gay rights, Mr. Rogers said. Though such cases—an arrest for soliciting sex in the men's room of the Minneapolis airport in Mr. Craig's case—have an initial ick factor to them, Mr. Rogers said they ultimately undermine antigay activists and politicians.

"It does help discredit them," he said.

| "Until acceptance is fully realized, we should continue to applaud each and every coming out as someone being true to themselves."

Celebrities Coming Out Helps Gay Rights

Trish Bendix

Trish Bendix is the managing editor of AfterEllen.com. In the following viewpoint, she argues that even though there is more acceptance of gay and lesbian individuals now than in the past, it is still important when celebrities come out. She argues that gay and lesbian youth need role models to show them that their sexuality is acceptable. She acknowledges that celebrities coming out will not necessarily convince homophobic people to change their minds. However, she argues that celebrities coming out can help inspire and inform gay and lesbian people. She concludes that society should celebrate everyone who is able to be true to themselves about their sexuality.

As you read, consider the following questions:

1. According to Bendix, when people talk about their coming out journey, what kind of anecdote will they often share?

2. Why and about what does Bendix disagree with Dan Savage?

3. In what kind of world does Bendix say she would like to live?

I'm generally quite happy with how the *New York Times* covers coming out and LGBT [lesbian, gay, bisexual, and transgender] issues. It's pretty much the reason I subscribe to the Sunday *Times*—I'm usually rewarded with at least a few gay news tips or stories, like recent features on [the film] *The Kids Are All Right* and the science of homosexual animals.

So I have to say I was a little perturbed with this weekend's story, ["Coming Out: When Love Dares Speak, and Nobody Listens"]. Mostly because I disagree with some of their major points.

Everybody Who Comes Out Matters

First, I would like to echo what Heather Hogan wrote about [country singer] Chely Wright when she first came out earlier this month [in May 2010], and has continued to write about as Chely makes her press rounds: Everyone's coming out matters. Even if you had no idea who Chely was before she came out, now you do, right? She's gay, she's advocating for the mental health and wellness of others in the closet so that they feel comfortable coming out and not living a lie like she had for so many years. I hope you wouldn't dismiss that.

The *Times* writes that "Americans greeted [Chely's coming out] largely with a shrug." Which could be true—I'm not sure who they surveyed, but it seems to me that there was equal shrugging with a whole lot of supportive and new fans of

Chely's. There were also a lot of preexisting fans that swore her off for being a lesbian. All of these people count, too.

If we discount her coming out, or [singer] Ricky Martin or [actor] Sean Hayes, for that matter, we're saying you shouldn't bother coming out unless you are going to make an impact. So, only if you're shocking—like the president or [actress] Julia Roberts maybe.

But the article's main point isn't that these celebrities (Chely, Ricky, etc.) shouldn't come out—it's that the general public doesn't care. It doesn't have an effect on their tolerance of gay people, should they not have any already. Writer Eric Marcus told the *Times*:

> There's the assumption among gay people that if only this famous person came out, things would be better—and that's never been the case. The most significant effort any of us can make in moving the ball forward in terms of promoting awareness and acceptance of this issue is for those of us who are gay to come out to those closest to us. It isn't ultimately the celebrity that changes people's minds, or the politician. It's the individual, one on one.

Inspire and Inform

I completely agree—coming out to the people in your lives (or, as [singer] Melissa Etheridge once said, even to the cashier at your grocery store) is important, but to say that public figures coming out makes less of an impact diminishes the idea that it makes an impact at all. Perhaps we are looking at this the wrong way: Are we expecting Chely Wright and Ricky Martin to make homophobic people become gay-friendly? You're right—that's not going to happen. But will these public figures and their words inspire and inform closeted youth and otherwise shamed or unsure gays, lesbians, bisexuals and everything under, in and around the rainbow? Yes, I'm quite sure of it.

If you ask most people about their coming out journey, so many of us will share an anecdote from pop culture. Depending on your generation, it could be the music of [singer] k.d. lang, or seeing the first televised lesbian kiss on *L.A. Law*. It could be [actor] Ellen's [referring to Ellen DeGeneres] coming out, Shakespeare's cross-dressing gender play in *Twelfth Night*, *The L Word* [a television show focused on lesbian characters] or when you first learned [actress] Marlene Dietrich wasn't just into men's suits.

Something, somewhere in society had an impact on you. Somehow you learned what gay was, an idea of how to be gay, who else was gay, that gay exists and you are not alone. No matter who you are, you have been affected by the media, entertainment, culture and society at large, and we are all informed by the same people, places and things. It's inevitable that someone coming out or kissing another girl or discussing sexual fluidity in a big, publicized way is going to affect you, consciously or otherwise.

The *Times* notes that a survey found "79 percent of respondents said that knowing someone who is gay contributed to their more positive opinions. Thirty-four percent who said seeing gay characters on television was a factor." I understand math, sir, and I'd like to say that I'll take that 34 percent and attempt to raise it with even more visibility of lesbians on television, thank you very much.

Don't Judge Coming Out

Another facet of the argument: Gay celebrities just want money and more fame. They waited until it was "safe" for them to come out. Dan Savage said:

> With more and more gays and lesbians coming out in middle school and high school, it's hard not to view coming out post-peak in your career or whenever as cowardly, if not opportunistic. Now that I have my millions, now that it's totally safe, now that I can scoop up a few more fans, I will come out. Forgive me, but I have much more admiration for those kids coming out in middle school.

Chely Wright Comes Out

I'd been in hiding most of my life and worked hard to protect my secret. No one like me in country music has ever admitted his or her homosexuality. There are gays in Nashville, but as far as anyone is led to believe, they are not those of us on the magazine covers. There is a slight understanding that there are gay publicists, songwriters, hair and makeup artists in the country music industry who help sell "straight" stars to the public, but that's it. And even among them, few are truly out of the closet.

I was a successful recording artist, a video star. I'd made *People* magazine's 50 Most Beautiful People list. Men in the armed forces asked me to autograph their Chely Wright posters. I'd been seen around town with a host of famous men—Brad Paisley, Vince Gill, Troy Aikman, and Brett Favre.

How could I be gay? Well, I am.

Chely Wright, Like Me:
Confessions of a Heartland Country Singer.
New York: Knopf Doubleday Publishing, 2010.

Dan Savage is not someone I usually disagree with, but this is an exception. When we start judging people's individual comings out, we do ourselves a disservice. We are saying that those who come out later in life are less authentic, or somehow less brave. Chely Wright faces just as many (if not more) skeptics and hateful people as children, but that aside, she spoke out on *Oprah* [*The Oprah Winfrey Show*] that those kids are the reason she felt it was necessary to come out now. She doesn't want them to go through what she did—the shame, the self-loathing, the straight sex. Does she stand to profit off of coming out while releasing a new album and book? Sure—but she also stands to lose profit from fans that refuse to give money to a now-gay country singer.

And what did [actress] Anna Paquin have to gain from coming out as bisexual in a PSA [public service announcement] for gay equality? Considering she's immensely successful and not selling anything, I'd imagine she's only going to bring awareness to the cause. And [comedian] Wanda Sykes? By coming out, she helped draw greater attention to the fight against Prop. 8 [referring to California Proposition 8, an anti-same-sex ballot initiative in California].

So you want to change someone's mind about homosexuality? Come out to them. Tell them you exist. But we should still support those who are in the position of helping the gay community stay visible and reach the LGBT community who doesn't feel part of a community yet. It's not an either/or thing. Don't tell me that the perceived success or amount of celebrity someone holds makes their sexuality matter to you more or less.

I would love to live in a world where no one has to come out—where we all just exist and our sexuality develops naturally, without question from anyone, and we all accept sexual fluidity for what it is—alive and well in everyone. Unfortunately, we live in a time where we have to tell our friends, family and grocery clerks that we're gay and proud, and have to hope that they'll accept that. Until acceptance is fully realized, we should continue to applaud each and every coming out as someone being true to themselves. That is always cause for celebration.

"The dialogue that surrounds the 'are you a feminist' question is far more important than whether pop culture icons actually identify as feminists."

Why We Need to Ask Celebrities Whether They're Feminists

Amanda Duberman

Amanda Duberman is the news editor for HuffPost Women. In the following viewpoint, she argues that it is useful to ask celebrities whether or not they are feminists. She contends that there are many misconceptions about feminism, and the dialogue prompted by celebrity answers is useful. For instance, many celebrities say they are not feminists because they don't hate men. Duberman argues that, in fact, feminism is not about hating men; it is about promoting equality. Celebrity confusion about the term is therefore a good way to have a discussion about what feminism really is and why people should support it.

As you read, consider the following questions:

1. According to Duberman, what did Shailene Woodley answer when asked if she was a feminist?

2. What does Duberman say is the generally agreed upon definition of feminism?

3. Why does Rhian Sasseen argue that female celebrities are unlikely to provide useful feminist dialogue?

Want to make your boring celebrity interview go viral in one easy step? Ask your subject if she's a feminist—the media loves a young ingénue denouncing the "-ism" du jour.

"Why" Is Important

When *Time* magazine asked [actress] Shailene Woodley if she was a feminist in May [of 2014], the *Divergent* star replied: "No because I love men, and I think the idea of 'raise women to power, take the men away from the power' is never going to work out because you need balance."

Her response predictably set off a veritable media frenzy. The backlash prompted Daily Beast reporter Marlow Stern to write that the question itself is "loaded" and "if you say you're not a feminist these days, the pitchforks come out."

Is the "are you or aren't you" question low-hanging fruit, employed to catch celebrities in the act just to get some buzz? Sometimes. But those of us interested in productive dialogue aren't critical of women for saying "I'm not a feminist," but for what they say after "*because*."

When we ask high-profile women if they are feminists, we can celebrate and promote their allegiance to a pretty agreeable principle, or discuss their reasoning for rejecting it. The "what" is the headline, but the "why" is the teachable moment.

Too many women still acknowledge a culture-wide misinterpretation of feminism, but when given opportunities to clarify and contextualize contemporary feminism, they instead blame the culture for revoking their right to claim it. Other female celebs find the term feminist "too strong" or think it has a "negative connotation." [Singer] Lady Gaga and Co. subscribe to the "liking men" and "embracing feminism" as mutually exclusive theory. Oh, and according to [singer] Lana del Rey, "the issue of feminism is just not an interesting concept."

Rejecting "feminism" for "humanism" is a vestigial tick, left over from a generation when feminism felt too radical and alienating. In the past few years, "feminism" has undergone a semantic evolution (or devolution, depending on your outlook) in pop culture. Its affiliation with political activism and ivory tower philosophy persists—as it should—but feminism has long entered the mainstream. The generally agreed upon definition of a feminist, said by Nigerian author Chimamanda Ngozi Adichie and christened by Beyoncé, is a "person who believes in the social, political and economic equality of the sexes."

Feminism and the Mainstream

The case could be made that such a broad definition of feminism neutralizes its more ambitious elements. But distilling it into a compact, largely unimpeachable dose served with a spoonful of sexy ladies (and gents) certainly makes the medicine go down a bit easier—which is exactly why there's even more of a story when it doesn't.

Woodley's rejection of feminism was particularly jarring. A woman evolved enough to fashion shampoo from the forest, challenge beauty standards and consistently choose dynamic female roles seems like she should be on board with feminism. But should we even care what she says?

At Salon, Rhian Sasseen argued against elevating celebrities to political icons. She pointed out that female celebrities are required to meet certain standards antagonistic to feminism. As such, they are poor vessels for meaningful feminist dialogue.

But aspiring to celebrity, and enduring the pressure to maintain it, does not absolve our public figures from explaining their philosophical positions. It endows them with the responsibility to do so.

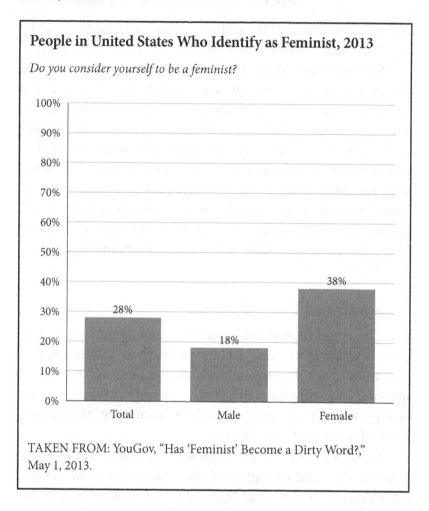

People in United States Who Identify as Feminist, 2013

Do you consider yourself to be a feminist?

TAKEN FROM: YouGov, "Has 'Feminist' Become a Dirty Word?," May 1, 2013.

The problem, of course, is when public figures incorrectly present their beliefs as being in opposition to the tenets of feminism. Saying you're not a feminist because it's not sisterhood is like saying you don't like Hawaii because it's cold. Homegirl, you've got it all wrong. *And someone should tell you.* Women's professed alternatives to feminism—e.g. "sisterhood" or "humanism"—are often its fundamental basis.

There are media outlets who will manipulate celebrities' misinterpretations of feminism for cheap clicks. Still, asking celebs if they are feminists sniffs some out from the cozy, noncommittal grey area between "feminist" and "not a feminist" long enough for us to show that such a place doesn't actually exist.

If the only legitimate completion of "I'm not a feminist because" is "I do not believe in the social, political, and economic equality of women," every report of a female celebrity—young ingénue or Hollywood pillar—sidestepping feminism to avoid man-hating or political posturing is an occasion to remind those listening where the movement truly begins. When Shailene Woodley said she didn't identify as a feminist because she "loves men," it became an opportunity to explain why hating men has nothing to do with feminism.

The Dialogue Is Important

The dialogue that surrounds the "are you a feminist" question is far more important than whether pop culture icons actually identify as feminists. Every answer given is an opportunity to discuss and clarify the term's truest meaning, inch the movement into more neutral territory and promote a deeper understanding of its core tenets. "Do you consider yourself a feminist" doesn't deserve to be a "loaded" question.

In Marlow Stern's recent interview with Shailene Woodley, they seemed to agree that critiquing a female celebrity for saying she is not a feminist amounts to a violation of "sisterhood." "The word 'feminist' is a word that discriminates, and I'm not into that," Woodley told Stern. "I don't think there has to be a separation in life in anything."

The word feminist only has the power to "discriminate" between those who believe in a basic equality and those who don't. There isn't much that differentiates a feminist from a decent human being. Every chance we have to make that clear, we should take.

"What's with so many interviewers asking female musicians or actresses about feminism? Why not just ask a feminist?"

Asking Female Celebrities If They Are Feminists Is Useless

Meghan Murphy

Meghan Murphy is the founder and editor of Feminist Current *blog and has written for the* Globe and Mail, Ms. *magazine, and Al Jazeera. In the following viewpoint, she argues that celebrities are not experts on feminism and often know little about it; therefore, asking a celebrity if she is a feminist is counterproductive. Often, Murphy says, celebrity discussions of feminism are ignorant and confused, and they simply add to popular myths and confusion surrounding feminism. She concludes that it would be best to stop asking celebrities about feminism, since they know and care little about it.*

As you read, consider the following questions:

1. Why does Murphy say that Kelis's "Milkshake" was not empowering?

2. According to Murphy, how does the idea that men and women should have different roles lead people to oppose feminism?

3. Who does Murphy say she will ask if she wants to learn about feminism?

I think maybe it's time to stop asking celebrities if they are feminist or not. If they don't do feminist work, what's the point? It's like asking me about Judaism or the raw food movement—I have no opinion and if you force me to come up with one I'm going to come off as an idiot. Those are not my areas of expertise. Lots of areas are not my areas of expertise.

Celebrities Aren't Experts in Feminism

What's with so many interviewers asking female musicians or actresses about feminism? Why not just ask a feminist? The vast majority of the time they have no real answer, don't seem to understand the meaning of the word, and then end up being pushed into controversy because they made some stupid/offensive statement about not being feminist because they "love men" (à la [singer] Lady Gaga). If the purpose of these interviews is to convince me that celebrities are just not all that smart, then fine. I believe you.

But if not, I don't know, maybe we need to stop asking them to form opinions on political movements when they really don't have any.

Kelis and Feminism

In an interview published at *Spin* today, [singer] Kelis was asked: "Songs like 'Milkshake,' 'Trick Me,' and 'Bossy' made you this empowered female figure to a generation for women. Would you consider yourself a feminist?"

First of all, what?? In what universe was "Milkshake" empowering for a generation of women?

My milkshake brings all the boys to the yard/And they're like/It's better than yours/Damn right it's better than yours/I can teach you/But I have to charge.

First of all, that song was annoying as hell. Second, teaching women that their sexuality is a commodity is not empowering.

Kelis responds to the interviewer by saying:

I've always shied away from the word "feminism," only because I think to truly be feminist I think it's a word that's unnecessary. I don't have to stamp it on my forehead or pass out T-shirts to prove that I'm happy to be a woman, or that I feel like I deserve equal rights.

For my generation and for your generation, I'm not negating the fight that women made before us. It's the same thing as when you talk about civil rights.

Well, are things perfect right now? Hell no. Is there still racism in a lot of the world? Absolutely. But the same fight is the fight of change. I don't feel the need to walk around with a rifle. It's just not beneficial; it doesn't make any sense. And for me, I feel like that puts us as women back. I'm in no way, shape, or form ignoring the fact that these things were astronomical in our world and they were necessary because people were smart, and brave, and powerful. But in this year, right now—yeah, do we get paid less than guys do? Sure. Is it equal? No. Should it be? Absolutely.

I'm not here to dis Kelis. All I'm saying is that it's clear she doesn't really get why feminism exists or what it is, so why lob the question her way? In fact, it seems like she's got a fairly conservative view of the roles men and women should play in this world.

So am I a feminist? I don't know. Call it what you want. I am extraordinarily happy to be a woman. I would not change it for the world. I think men should run the world because if not there would be no balance. Men cannot have children, they will never know what that feels like. To actually have life—to give birth and life to someone. If we ran the entire world also, we would annihilate. There would be no balance whatsoever. So I'm fine with that. If men want to run the world, great. Congratulations. If that makes you feel equal to those that can actually create life. But I don't care. There are so many more important things to think about. I feel like people are constantly complaining about injustice. And like I said, it's different than when we had to fight to vote, okay? But right now, if you want to be a successful woman, are there going to be challenges? Yeah. But so what? It's possible, it's possible. You know. Be a woman and make it happen. Just do what you have to do. I feel like all my friends, my sisters, my mom, my aunts and all the people who I value, they're brilliant. And are they aware of the fact that things might be a little skewed? Yeah. But it doesn't make them any less awesome or capable. All these titles are just so useless.

Contributing to Confusion

A lot of people learn that men and women should have different roles in this world in order to create "balance" and, therefore, end up with this idea that feminism is not only "anti-man" but "anti-woman" because it's "against" femininity (or masculinity). If you think that masculine and feminine gender roles are not only innate but good, then you're likely to see critiques of those gender roles as attacking actual males and females, rather than attacking those socialized roles and behaviours, as well as the hierarchy that is attached to said roles. This leads women to say things like "No, I'm not a feminist, I love being a woman," because they believe their womanhood is attached to a subordinate gender role which they have been told is not only natural, but empowering.

It seems to me that asking celebrities to talk about feminism only contributes to the mass confusion around what feminism actually is (Is it about feeling "empowered?" Is it about hating men? Is it about equality? Is it about being a lesbian? Is it about labels? Is it about being angry all the time?) and causes controversy as people feel disappointed when their idols turn out to be not all that smart or progressive.

[Country singer] Taylor Swift responded to the question "Do you consider yourself a feminist?" by saying "I don't really think about things as guys versus girls." [Pop singer] Björk took the old *I'm more into positivity than negativity* route, reinforcing the notion that fighting patriarchy is just about a bunch of angry, whiny women who hate everything (and should just *think positive!*). [Pop singer] Geri Halliwell bought into the idea that "feminism is bra-burning lesbianism" and therefore "very unglamorous," suggesting a "rebrand" that celebrates "femininity and softness." Famous burlesque dancer [and model] Dita Von Teese just seems totally and completely confused, saying: "It's not a word I don't really like to address, you know? It's not even that I want to call myself that. I just sort of go, 'Oooooh!' It's an eyeball roller, (*laughs*) You know what I mean? It's like, oh man, it's a weird question. The word "feminist" is so broad." . . . Come again?

This list could go on, but you get the picture. The question seems worthwhile if the goal is to educate, but that doesn't seem to be the point when these stereotypical, antifeminist, or nonsensical answers are just left hanging out there. Who cares what celebrities think about feminism? They didn't become pop stars because of their deep commitment to social justice (though if they happen to be both a celebrity and committed to social justice, great). If I want to learn about feminism, I'll go ask a feminist. Just like if I want to learn about veganism or climate change or physics, I'll go ask an expert, not some rando [random person] on the street and certainly not some twentysomething pop star.

> *"Music videos are only a small compo-*
> *nent of the 'wallpaper' of supposedly*
> *dangerous images surrounding children,*
> *but they are one of the few areas of the*
> *media that remain unregulated."*

Children Provide the Excuse for Moral Panic Around Celebrity Culture

Karina Wilson

Karina Wilson is a story consultant, teacher, and writer working in the film industry. In the following viewpoint, she argues that concerns about the videos of pop star Rihanna are based on a moral panic. She says that worries about children being exposed to sexual content has been around for decades, but that it is always presented as new and as requiring regulation. She says that Rihanna's videos are being used as a way to demand that the music industry adopt a rating system for videos, though it is unclear how this will restrict children's access to videos online.

Karina Wilson, "Rihanna: Moral Panic Poster Child," Mediaknowall, June 3, 2011. Copyright © 2011 by Mediaknowall. All rights reserved. Reproduced by permission.

As you read, consider the following questions:

1. What aspects of Rihanna's personal life have made her videos about sex and violence especially controversial, according to Wilson?

2. What is the Mothers' Union, according to the viewpoint?

3. According to Wilson, what has Rihanna said in response to the controversy about her videos?

R ihanna's new music video release, "Man Down," coincides with calls in the UK [United Kingdom] for a music video rating system to protect younger viewers from adult content. In the opening sequence of the video, she shoots a man—who is later revealed to be her attacker—in the street. Given that this comes hot on the heels of the controversy surrounding the sexual content of her last video, "S&M," the cumulative outcome is that Rihanna becomes the poster child for this latest moral panic about media effects, whether she likes it or not.

Stages of Moral Panic

We can see all three formal stages of a moral panic illustrated nicely here.

1. Occurrence and signification

Rihanna is a female pop star who goes on the record as saying she suffered abuse as a child. In 2009, she was also involved in a domestic violence situation with then boyfriend Chris Brown, for which he was sentenced to five years' probation; the drama of the assault, arrest and sentencing are all played out in the public eye. Therefore, when she releases a series of videos that speak to the topics of sex and violence ("Love the Way You Lie," "S&M," "Man Down"), the media exploit the personal angle, and devote many column inches to exploring the connection between Rihanna's life and her songs. Rihanna's raunchy performance on *The X Factor* in December

Moral Panics

The *moral panic* is a scare about a threat or supposed threat from deviants or "folk devils," a category of people who, presumably, engage in evil practices and are blamed for menacing a society's culture, way of life, and central values. The word "scare" implies that the concern over, fear of, or hostility toward the folk devil is *out of proportion* to the actual threat that is claimed.

Who exactly has to be scared to qualify a scare as a panic? Is it the whole society, or simply a part of it? How scared do they have to be? What do they get scared about? And just what is it that they do when they're expressing that panic? Does the general public have to be scared, or can the "scare" be confined to expressions of fear in the mass media, or to a small collectivity within the society at large?

Some supposed threats are, evidence suggests, entirely imaginary. Carefully and systematically weighed, available data indicate that satanic ritual abuse did not take place, that aliens have *not* abducted humans, and that "snuff" movies [in which deaths are filmed] are the stuff of urban legends. There is, in other words, a *delusional* aspect to moral panics. In other moral panics, the supposed threat may be genuine, even harmful, but the alarm raised is disproportionate to that threat. . . . Even if approximately true, a claim may be *exaggerated*: perhaps the number of victims, or the financial cost to society, or how widespread the harm is, or the inevitability of the causal sequence from less to more harmful threats—any of these could be inflated above and beyond what the evidence, carefully assessed, indicates.

Erich Goode and Nachman Ben-Yehuda,
Moral Panics: The Social Construction of Deviance.
Malden, MA: Blackwell, 2009.

2010 is the subject of several complaints to Ofcom [Office of Communications in the United Kigdom], garnering further headlines. Rihanna's star persona is therefore a combination of elements, from the sexy projections in her performances to the vulnerability she displays in her very public personal life. She is both victim and temptress: News outlets can use her any way they want.

2. Wider social implications (fanning the flames)

Rihanna's videos coincide with growing fears about the over-sexualisation of children. This fear derives from advertising, clothing, books, TV, movies and music aimed at preteens. In April 2011, Reg Bailey, head of the Mothers' Union (a Christian group) in the UK claims that parents are

> "struggling against the slow creep of an increasingly commercial and sexualised culture and behaviour, which they say prevents them from parenting the way they want.... [They have] little faith in regulators or businesses taking their concerns seriously."

BBC News (among other outlets) reports:

> A survey carried out for the review suggested that almost nine out of 10 UK parents thought children were having to grow up too early....

> A majority of parents of five- to 16-year-olds said music videos and a "celebrity culture" were encouraging children to act older than they were.

Rihanna's image and videos are used to illustrate news stories about the moral dangers of overly sexualised pop music (which has been perceived as a problem since the jazz age), although there is no evidence that her output has a particular impact upon young minds.

3. Social controls

Thanks to the work and recommendations of Reg Bailey and the Mothers' Union, an official government policy is to give music video broadcasters eighteen months to come up with a voluntary code that will rate music videos on a content basis and restrict broadcast times accordingly. This coincides with record label boss Richard Russell's proclamation that Adele's success is based on her specifically non-outrageous, non-sexual image, which suggests that public opinion is no longer in favor of sexy female pop stars like Rihanna.

Ineffective Regulation

Music videos are only a small component of the "wallpaper" of supposedly dangerous images surrounding children, but they are one of the few areas of the media that remain unregulated—therefore they make an appropriate target for social control. News stories imply the tide is turning against explicitly sexual and violent music videos, and vulnerable 5–16-year-olds will no longer be able to watch them on TV before 9pm. Phew! Problem solved, moral panic over.

However, BBC News duly notes:

> Campaigners will scrutinise the full recommendations when they are published to see how effective they might be in the digital age, when most young people view music videos online and on their telephones.

And, on June 2, a bemused Rihanna, who is only making pop music to entertain people the best way she knows how, tweets:

> I'm a 23-year-old rockstar with NO KIDS! What's up with everybody wantin me to be a parent? I'm just a girl, I can only be your/our voice!

Periodical and Internet Sources Bibliography

The following articles have been selected to supplement the diverse views presented in this chapter.

Seth Adam	"Celebrities Sound Off Against Homophobia After Fallen Teen Idol Kirk Cameron Launches Anti-Gay Attack," GLAAD, March 5, 2012.
Kim Allen, Laura Harvey, and Heather Mendick	"Is Celebrity Culture Really That Bad for Our Students?," *Guardian*, November 16, 2012.
Harry Belafonte	"Black Artists Must Do More," Daily Beast, September 2, 2012.
Chronicle (Duke University)	"Celebrity Feminism, Tune In," September 3, 2014.
Joan E. Greve	"17 Famous Women on What Feminism Means to Them," *Time*, June 23, 2014.
Holly Hamilton-Bleakley	"Out of the Cave: Leading Our Children Away from Celebrity Culture," *MercatorNet*, July 2, 2014.
Malia Jacobson	"The Miley Effect: Do Celebrities Shape Kids' Values?," *ParentMap* (Washington State), October 25, 2013.
Emilee Lindner	"16 Celebs Who Aren't Afraid to Call Themselves Feminists," MTV News, May 30, 2014.
Mychal Denzel Smith	"Jay-Z and the Politics of Celebrity," *ThinkProgress*, September 6, 2012.
Laurence Watts	"Talented People Should Not Fear Coming Out," *Huffington Post*, November 14, 2011.
Andi Zeisler	"Let's Not Fawn over Male Celebrity Feminists: Making Stars Weigh In on Women's Rights Is Hurting the Cause," Salon, August 20, 2014.

 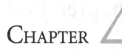

Is Celebrity Culture Changing?

Chapter Preface

Celebrity endorsements are changing in some important ways. In the past, celebrities might just appear in an advertisement or two for a brand, without any long-term commitment. In part because of social media and online connections, consumers now expect to be able to interact more broadly, and more constantly, with brands and with celebrity endorsers, according to Caroline McCarthy in a December 2011 post on the Think with Google website. McCarthy says:

> We're seeing a trend of celebrities, when becoming the spokesperson or "face" of a brand, taking on titles like investors, creative directors, and advisors that imply a much deeper level of involvement than simply being in a cosmetics company's ads. Lady Gaga isn't just the poster girl of camera brand Polaroid, she's its "creative director,".... And in a twist that eschews the classic model of the celebrity being the one getting compensated, entertainment figures like MC Hammer, Alyssa Milano, and (most famously) Ashton Kutcher have begun making venture capital investments in new companies, becoming involved not just as financial backers but as already-recognizable celebrity spokespeople.

Samantha Turtle at the PRNews website agrees, noting that "celebrity endorsements as we've known them are undergoing a transformation, from one-and-done deals to more authentic, long-term and immersive relationships." She adds that "as relationships between celebrities and companies evolve and deepen, we are seeing celebrity and brand relationships evolve from dating towards marriage." By associating themselves closely with a celebrity, brands can increase name recognition and promote themselves more effectively to the celebrity's fans. For their part, the celebrities stand to gain more in money and exposure themselves, especially if the brand does well.

The Associated Press's Christina Rexrode reports at Yahoo News that celebrities have also begun to endorse products through social media. Celebrities can have huge Twitter followings, and a celebrity tweet is relatively cheap compared to an ad campaign. Reality television personality Khloé Kardashian charged $8,000 for a tweet and has promoted Old Navy through her Twitter account. Singer Ray J, who has more than six hundred thousand Twitter followers, endorsed the movie *Saw 3D* on the social media site; his rate is around $2,300 a tweet. "Of course," Rexrode says, "anything on Twitter is short-lived and reaches only a small, self-selecting audience: Research firm eMarketer estimates that only 11 percent of US adult Internet users are on the micro-blogging site. And even though some celebs have faithful groups of followers, it can be hard to measure whether their tweets lead people to spend." Still, as more and more people spend time online and skip television ads with DVD recorders, marketers are looking for new ways to reach their audiences, and celebrity tweets are one new tool they can use.

The viewpoints in the following chapter explore ways in which celebrity is changing, focusing on such issues as the way social media has, or has not, allowed fans to get closer to celebrities and whether celebrity culture is more prevalent today than it was in the past.

| "For [Lady] Gaga, fame is an internal
| process."

Celebrity Culture Can Become More Accessible and Subversive

Amber L. Davisson

Amber L. Davisson is an assistant professor of rhetoric and media studies at Willamette University in Salem, Oregon. In the following viewpoint, she discusses pop singer Lady Gaga's idea and use of fame. Gaga argues that fame is not something granted by others, but it is an internal state of believing in oneself. Davisson describes Gaga's enthusiastic promotion of her own fans through social media and other venues as an example of the way in which the singer makes fame individual and communal at the same time. Davisson argues that Gaga's redefinition of fame is potentially carnivalesque and subversive.

As you read, consider the following questions:

1. According to the viewpoint, what is the Feast of Fools?

2. How does Lady Gaga define "the fame," according to the viewpoint?

3. How has Lady Gaga used the idea of paparazzi to promote her fans, according to Davisson?

Lady Gaga preaches fame as a choice and a way of being—accessible through personal decisions and separate from the status that comes from mainstream media attention. As she puts it, "it's a sharable fame: I want to invite you all to the party, I want people to feel a part of this lifestyle." This does not mean that everyone should seek celebrity status from the media, although that has been traditionally held as the main way to acquire celebrity in American culture. In fact, Gaga's notion of celebrity denies the media's jurisdiction over deciding who is famous and who is not. It also questions the way money and possessions are used by the media as status symbols:

> Fame is not pretending to be rich, it's carrying yourself in a way that exudes confidence and passion for music or art or fishing or whatever the hell it is that you're passionate about, and projecting yourself in a way that people say, "Who the f--- is that?" It has nothing to do with money. I can wear a $2 pair of pants and a T-shirt and a pair of sunglasses for two bucks on the street, but I can make it look like I'm [wealthy socialite] Paris Hilton. You gotta have the fame, you gotta exude that thing. You gotta make people care, you gotta know and believe how important you are. You gotta have conviction in your ideas.

Fame and Carnival

Traditionally, celebrities have fed consumer culture by convincing people that material goods were necessary status symbols. These ideas of celebrity being rooted in wealth and possessions rely on something external to validate one's sense of self. For Gaga, fame is an internal process. She invites her fans "to walk around delusional about how great they can be, and then to fight so hard for it every day that the lie becomes the truth." The delusion includes eschewing the trappings of consumer culture in favor of developing a sense of self. This way of discussing fame echoes Mikhail Bakhtin's arguments about carnival.

In his writings on François Rabelais, a French Renaissance satirist known for bawdy jokes and grotesque humor, Mikhail Bakhtin places the origins of carnival at a medieval festival known as the Feast of Fools. According to Bakhtin, this was a space where the social norms of a society were turned upside down. In Europe, during medieval times, the church and the government exercised an extreme amount of power over people's daily lives. This, combined with harsh economic conditions, made citizens restless. The Feast of Fools offered a brief, albeit church-sanctioned, revolution. Citizens were given license to express all the dissent and unrest they normally suppressed—including mocking the sexual habits of priests and parodying the behavior of bishops. Typical communication practices were cast aside to create a level of familiarity in language that would not have been seen in traditional conversation. Unlike other festivals or public performances, "carnival is not a spectacle seen by the people; they live in it, and everyone participates because its very idea embraces all the people." This festival was a place of escapism and a release valve for pent-up frustrations.

Gaga's fame embraces the spirit of escapism and the subversion of social norms: "The 'notion' of escapism may be a lie, but for some of us this lie is our truth. You must desire the reality of fantasy so profusely that it becomes necessity, not accessory." This lie forms the basis for Gaga's relationship with her fans, the little monsters. At the start of each concert on the Monster Ball Tour, Gaga read the *Manifesto [of Little Monsters]*, which stated: "It is in the theory of perception that we have established our bond, or the lie I should say, for which we kill. We are nothing without our image, without our projection; without the spiritual hologram of who we perceive ourselves to be or rather to become, in the future." The fame Gaga advocates is a modern Feast of Fools. It is a space to ignore the rigid social hierarchies established by the media and create a new reality.

During the medieval Feast of Fools, the traditional audience-speaker power relationship was forgone in favor of an almost abrasive casualness that pulled the audience into dialogue with the speaker. Performers would shout profanities at viewers until the audience was forced to give up their role as passive watchers and return the abuse. Bakhtin points to footlights as a primary element that differentiated carnival from other types of public performances at the time. In the theaters of that era, footlights were lamps traditionally placed at the base of the stage, with their light shining on the thing perceived as deserving of attention. The lights created a distinction: On one side of the footlight would be the audience sitting in darkness and on the other side is the performance, illuminated, for everyone to see. In carnival there is no footlight. There is no audience. There is no performer. The whole of the festival was part of the show. Today the mass media often functions like a footlight; it shines a light on celebrities, so it is clear who is the audience and who is the performer. Gaga is arguing for a new carnival-like atmosphere. One where everyone should ignore that footlight and embrace a world where they are no longer audience but celebrity.

Fame and Subversion

While the notion of a sharable fame might sound harmless—just a bunch of teenage girls strutting around their high school declaring themselves celebrities—it contains the possibility of a much larger disruption of authority. Typically, the media controls the major outlets of popular expression, deciding who is worthy of public attention and who is granted fame.

Gaga's message raises questions about where fame comes from: "What I want to deliver, as a message about fame, is that anyone can have it. My fame lives in my friendships, in my convictions about the power of art and love." That attitude creates a space similar to the one Bakhtin described. Within this environment, "whatever the authority of a discourse, those who are seeing it as an image, as a mask that has been revealed to be a mask, now have the capacity to judge whether it represents their own condition." Carnival communication has an informal quality; "when two persons establish friendly relations, the form of their verbal intercourse also changes abruptly; they address each other informally, abusive words are used affectionately, and mutual mockery is permitted." The carnival assumes this friendly relationship between the speaker and the audience. Profanity or abuse could be taken as spectacular within commonplace entertainment, but within the familiarity and intimacy of carnival communication they take on an "ambivalence." Lady Gaga speaks to her fans with familiarity, calling them her "little monsters." She attributes her success to their dedication as much as her own and holds them in the regard of family.... These moments of blurring the power relationship between celebrity and spectator integrate into the notion of sharable fame as the motivation behind the carnivalesque style. Robert Hariman describes this as one of the functions of the carnival performance, pulling the rhetoric down and "casting that image before the most democratic, undisciplined, and irreverent conception of a public audience." Carnival does not mimic lived experience exactly; it places the absurd in the context of lived experience.

Gaga's rhetorical choice not to move back and forth between real life and stage life constructs her performance as an immersive experience. This move is part of her overall concept of *the* fame, which she distinguishes as something apart from the typical mainstream media notion of fame. Gaga explains that the "fame, which I'm experiencing now, is very different from *the fame*. The fame is when nobody knows who you are but everybody wants to know who you are. I still experience a lot of that." The fame is treated not as a status, or a line that is crossed, but as a daily choice. Generally, fame is about celebrity status and media recognition: "That kind of fame, to me, is the kind of fame that everybody knows about, and the kind of fame that I write about is a very special kind of fame that I think is really positive and can affect people's lives in a really, really amazing way." A big part of what separates the two notions of fame is personal agency. One is about doing something that gets other people to recognize you as important, and the other is about recognizing that quality in yourself and embracing it. Gaga's conception of fame sets up a very different kind of power relationship between the performer and her fans. Rather than inviting them to mimic her, she is inviting them to find something great in themselves.

All of Gaga's work shows a unique relationship to the spectator. Her use of the carnivalesque style changes the nature of her public discourse. She still often wears the mask of spectacle, but she performs the mask in such a way that it alters its nature. With Gaga, the face behind the mask turns out to be the mask. As she puts it, "persona is the first word people think of when they're trying to figure out how to describe what it is that I do. . . . Gaga is not a character. . . . Everything you see is an extension of me. It's not a character that I play on television." This shift in expectation effectively changes the overall environment of the conversation she is having with her fans. As she puts it, "it's the context of what I'm doing that makes people concerned." This same behavior through a more traditional media outlet, separated from the user-generated content, would function to reinforce the footlights. When Lady Gaga performs it constantly and publicly it ceases to look like a mask and starts to look like the truth.

Lady Gaga, Marketer

I first became a Gaga fan in 2009 when I was drawn in by the addictive dance beats of her first album, *The Fame*. Yet the more I watched how she interacted with her fans, the more impressed I became with how she methodically created her passionate fan base. I saw her relate to her fans on a much more intimate level than most of her ego-driven contemporaries did. Fans were pouring their hearts out online, not just about how much they loved Gaga's music and fashion, but also about how she had inspired them to be better people. I wanted to know how she was inspiring such devotion. I read every article I could find about her and pored through interviews she had given to print and television outlets. I started following her on Facebook, where she has the third-highest number of fans with 55 million, and on Twitter, where she is the most followed with more than 33 million followers, as well as on Tumblr and other social sites. I watched grainy, tinny-sounding videos of her performances and concerts uploaded to YouTube by fans around the world. I visited the top Gaga fan sites daily to see what they were reporting and what fans were saying on the forums. I've even been to three of her concerts. What I began to see amazed me. Lady Gaga is doing something casual observers and many business professionals may not really comprehend. While creating a buzz with her wild outfits and crazy performance art, she is methodically building a grassroots base of passionate fans for the long term. The more I observed, the more I began to realize that there is a lot she could teach the business world about how to generate customer loyalty.

Jackie Huba, Monster Loyalty: How Lady Gaga Turns Followers into Fanatics. *New York: Penguin, 2013.*

Fame as Liberation

Lady Gaga has said that her ultimate goal is to live an identity that encourages fans to rethink how they express their own identities. In an interview with Barbara Walters, Gaga professed: "I aspire to try to be a teacher to my young fans ... who feel just like I felt when I was younger. ... I felt like a freak, I guess, what I'm trying to say is, I want to liberate them, I want to free them of their fears and make them feel ... that they can create their own space in the world." Part of that liberation is a sense of fame that is personal and close: "I want to give people the self-confidence and the sense of inner fame that I feel without being pummeled by the paparazzi as I walk down the street." When Gaga talks about fame, she draws some important distinctions between fame and modern celebrity culture. As mentioned before, traditional fame and celebrity are often attributed to those who possess characteristics that society considers worth glorifying. According to traditional standards, fame is defined by outside attention. Someone knows they are famous when the paparazzi are trying to catch their every move and media is scrutinizing those moves to decide if they live up to celebrity standards. Gaga is advocating a sense of fame that exists without outside validation. This sort of fame is liberating, because it is not predicated on trying to be worthy of media attention.

Often when Gaga articulates the meaning behind the fame, she uses metaphors of space and discusses it as an interaction with her fan community. By situating fame in the direct interaction between Gaga and her fans, she removes the mainstream media as the center of celebrity and refocuses the conversation in a way that changes the agency of both herself and her audience. Commenting on her album *The Fame*, Gaga said that "it's fame in the Warholian Studio 54 kind of way, not the stereotypical fame that people read about in tabloids and is considered very poisonous." She uses the metaphor of the famed Studio 54 [a New York nightclub of the 1970s] to delineate between her notion of fame and fame that comes from the media. That communal notion of fame, based on directly interacting with fans, requires an extreme openness and authenticity. Lady Gaga argues that there are ways for celebrities to be open with their fans, develop a community, without giving up a sense of self: "Part of my mastering of the art of fame, part of it is getting people to pay attention to what you want them to pay attention to. And not pay attention to the things you don't want them to pay attention to." This attitude definitely raises questions about the authenticity of Gaga's honesty with her fans. As she has explained, "My philosophy is that if I am open with them about everything, and yet I art direct every moment of my life, I can maintain a sort of privacy in a way. I maintain a certain soulfulness that I have yet to give." The argument she is making is that the performance of total honesty allows her to hold something back so she always has more to give. She manages to hold back while always appearing to give everything to her fans. Perhaps this is the lie of celebrity that Gaga so often talks about in interviews.

Inner fame comes without the specter of losing the "it" factor. Gaga's fans have embraced this philosophy. In an American *Vogue* interview with Jonathan Van Meter, Lady Gaga commented on the evolution of the nature of her fans: "Every show there's a little more eyeliner, a little more freedom, and a little more 'I don't give a f--- about the bullies at my school.'" Despite Gaga's movement into mainstream popular culture, "for some reason the fans didn't become more Top 40. They've become even more of this cult following." Ann T. Torrusio points out that "Gaga's fans always perceive her adoration for them as genuine, and it is possible that they may well be correct. However, it cannot be ignored that her well-cultivated relationship . . . has lured her 'Little Monsters' into the margins of culture." In her shows, Gaga constantly pushes to develop a relationship to the fans; "I am not going to saunter around the stage doing pelvic thrusts and lip-synching. . . .

I want to be your cool older sister who you feel really connected with, who you feel understands you and refuses to judge anything about you because she's been there." Being a Lady Gaga fan is not about embracing a trend; it is more about joining a community who actively declare themselves as living on the fringes of society.

Lady Gaga, Fan of Fans

The paparazzi are a critical part of the culture surrounding modern celebrities, and as part of her commitment to spreading fame Gaga enjoys playing paparazzi for her fans. After signing a major promotional deal with Polaroid, Lady Gaga began carrying around a camera and taking pictures of her fans everywhere she went. In 2012, Lady Gaga had more than 26 million followers on Twitter. So, when she plays paparazzi and posts a picture of her fans online that photo has almost as many viewers as a major magazine. Gaga's fans help to make her famous and she returns the favor. She does not stop at Twitter. In 2010, *V* magazine did an issue that was dedicated to the "new." As part of the issue, Gaga nominated the little monsters as the "new fan." The issue included collages and full-page photos assembled by Gaga, featuring fans posing in their various homages to the star. Gaga is promoting her fans through mainstream media outlets, and she is sharing the spotlight with them. Even in small ways, the Mother Monster likes to act as a fan of her fans. Lady Gaga told a reporter that at a concert in Japan "I brought my favorite pocketbook and I wanted all my Japanese fans to sign it, so I could always have you with me." Just like fans hound Gaga for autographs, she goes after them. Lady Gaga was upset because her Birkin bag was un-relatable, "[s]o how do I create it into something that they [her fans] will love and adore, and turn it into a performance-art piece in itself? My fans are more iconic than this purse. I love fashion, but I don't love it more than my fans. And that's what this bag is all about." The bag was covered in fan art from her tour in Japan and Taiwan. In September of 2012, Lady Gaga made a post to her YouTube account labeled "Oh! You Pretty Things," which is the title of the David Bowie song that provides the sound track for the video. The video was a series of short clips of fans, members of the Haus of Gaga, and paparazzi that Gaga had recorded while she was out on tour for *Born This Way*. Within only two days it had more than 62,000 views, and that number was continuing to grow. The behavior of playing paparazzi and getting fan autographs offers tangible reinforcement for Gaga's philosophy of fame. In her interactions with her fans, Lady Gaga mimics the way fans treat celebrities. This works to break down typical communication patterns in celebrity culture.

Lady Gaga combines the performance of the 24/7, "always on," celebrity with an intimate communication style to demonstrate that fame can be normalized. A major factor in this performance is a sense of honesty that goes past the traditional confessional celebrity moments. During an interview with Anderson Cooper on *60 Minutes*, Gaga said: "When you asked me about the sociology of fame and what artists do wrong, what artists do wrong is they lie. And I don't lie. I'm not a liar. I built good will with my fans. They know who I am. And I'm just like them in so many ways." . . . Gaga has lived her fame very publicly and treated her quest for celebrity as something she shares with her fans. For that to work, the interactions have to lose their staged confessional quality and become about real intimacy. The celebrity status that Gaga advocates is about a lifestyle: "I believe in living a glamorous life and I believe in a glamorous lifestyle. . . . What that means is not money or fame or prestige. It's a sense of vanity and glamour and subculture that is rooted in a sense of self. I am completely 100,000% devoted to a life of glamour." As she said after releasing *The Fame Monster*, it is all about "the dream of wanting to make something of yourself." The fame is about a sense of self and agency that cannot be granted or taken away by any media outlet.

This way of talking about fame is not wholly new. In fact, most people have experiences of interacting with small-scale fame and local celebrity in their day-to-day lives.

> "Although there is no imaginable future
> in which one can imagine an end to
> celebrity and fame and mass media at-
> tention, there is a prospect that the
> fame-inflation and boundary-blurring
> that has been happening over the past
> decade may finally be losing its impe-
> tus."

The Culture of Celebrity
Is Far from Dead—It's Just
Growing Up

Tim Lott

*Tim Lott is a British author. In the following viewpoint, he ar-
gues that celebrity is improving, in that talentless celebrities seem
to be diminishing in importance. He argues that celebrities who
have some useful talent or who have done something worthwhile
are becoming more prominent. He argues that this is a good
thing and that celebrity can be valuable when it brings fame to
talented people.*

As you read, consider the following questions:

1. What evidence does Lott present that certain kinds of celebrity are fading?

2. What is the reality of the secret of celebrity, according to Lott?

3. Why does Lott say that a reformed celebrity culture is better than no celebrity culture at all?

For snobs, aesthetes and elitists everywhere, something rather pleasing is emerging out of the lurid landscape of the mass media. The cult of celebrity is finally faltering. High profiles are descending. Fame in the marketplace is starting to carry a red cut-price sticker.

Is Celebrity Fading?

Waterstones' bookstores have reported that the latest batch of celebrity memoirs has failed so badly that the boss, who put his shirt on their success, has resigned. At the newsstands, celebrity magazines are showing a big year-on-year drop in readership. *Heat, Now* and *Hello!* have all registered significant slumps.

On the idiot box, *Celebrity Big Brother* [a reality show featuring celebrities] is in its final series and the producers have reached new lows of desperation to find anyone who will put themselves through it.

Could the public's love affair with celebrity finally be over? Will the time come when a prime minister will no longer publicly worry about the physical health of Jade Goody [a reality star who was diagnosed with cancer] and the mental health of [singer] Susan Boyle? Will the ransom we pay to celebrity no longer seem to be good value for money?

Well—up to a point. *OK!* magazine is still selling close on 600,000 a week, only a few thousand down on the 12 months previously. Last year's *I'm a Celebrity . . . Get Me Out of Here* was a big success for ITV. And even *Celebrity Big Brother* [CBB] is still producing respectable figures for Channel 4—maybe a million up on last year's nonentity *Big Brother.*

Celebrity Still Generates Profit

The long and short of it is that although the celebrity factor may be fading on some fronts, it still has too much worth in the marketplace to be allowed to fail. Global business interests are always going to devote vast resources to make sure that it maintains that worth, since celebrity generates so much profit. Damage celebrity culture and you damage vast swathes of sales of perfumes, magazines, handbags, designer labels for clothes and much else, at a stroke. Celebrity culture must continue, not least for purely economic reasons, and it will.

But business can't maintain the crop of celebrity in barren ground. The fascination is deeply rooted in us. Clearly, it answers a deep need, a religious need, almost. We need to worship and we need to crucify. This was true when our celebrities were kings and priests, rather than soap stars and reality TV characters.

There is another reason for celeb worship. We continue to watch celebrities because, it seems, they have a secret. They have a secret that makes them talented or famous or rich. We watch them in the strange hope that we can uncover their secret.

But the reality is that there is no secret—or not one that can be learnt. I have met enough people who are actually famous for being talented to know that talent and personality are very different things. A remarkable talent is rarely a remarkable person. Like evil, talent is often banal. And if this is true of the talented, then it is 10 times more true of the merely famous for being famous.

So much for the theory (and I do not deny that these explanations are not entirely novel). Out there in the real world, the fact is, parts of the celebrity machine are definitely starting to creak. There are certainly enough changes taking place in the celebosphere to at least give pause for thought. What would the world actually look like without celebrities? All snobbery aside, would we be actually better off without them?

I would like to admit first that I occasionally enjoy the spectacle of empty celebrity—my guilty pleasure in CBB cannot be denied—but I am chiefly in favour of people who are famous for their talent. It strikes me as a genuinely positive thing for people who have worked hard to nurture a particular ability to be held up as a role model, whether you are [soccer star] David Beckham (who is a celebrity) or [poet and playwright] Carol Ann Duffy (who is simply well known).

To clarify that distinction—what is the difference between the well-known, or famous, person and the celebrity? Beckham is a celebrity because he is glamorous, beautiful and rich. He especially appeals to young people and working-class people, which all tend to point in the direction of the "celebrity" definition.

His undoubted talent is what defines a clear line connecting him to Carol Ann Duffy. Duffy is famous because she has been honoured in her appointment as the Poet Laureate as a consequence of her great ability in her field, like Beckham. But she is merely famous—as opposed to being a "sleb"—because old people are probably more interested in her than young people, because she is not glamorous, because she is not rich. Her fame is of a different nature—one is unlikely to see her modelling swimwear. But it is equally well deserved, and doubtless somewhat welcome to her, at least in financial terms.

It is a good thing that poets can become famous in these modern media times. This points up a much ignored positive side of so-called "celebrity culture" (which I would prefer to think of as "fame culture", "celebrity" being a slightly different thing). It is easy to forget that many very talented individuals who would have otherwise been condemned to poverty-ridden obscurity have also been caught up in this fame net, alongside the nonentities and mass-marketed talents.

Poets such as Duffy and Simon Armitage, artists such as Grayson Perry and Rachel Whiteread, even talented classical performers Katherine Jenkins and Evelyn Glennie, all of whom would once have been condemned to popular obscurity, however privately admired, now get sufficient attention to help maintain a career or in some cases, even amass wealth.

Famous for Not Much

So much for the deservedly well known, whether sleb or famous. This brings us to another schism, those on the wrong side of which provoke much wailing and rending of clothes. These are the people who are famously famous for not very much. They are famous because they have appeared on reality TV shows, or because they are related to someone famous (Peaches Geldof [daughter of singer Bob Geldof]) or because they are unusually good-looking ([model] Kate Moss), or because they are rich and perform oral sex on the Internet (Paris Hilton) or they have some attractive deformity such as unusually large breasts ([singer and model] Jordan [aka Katie Price]). I would include the Royal Family in this category, but I recognise this may be an unpopular view.

It is in this third category, where talent or effort seem only remotely connected to fame, that appears, encouragingly, to be wilting. Nonentity *Big Brother* has been pulled because of the lack of interest in its participants. *Wife Swap* has also gone. Jordan's memoir is one of the books that performed badly over Christmas.

The pattern is clear. Although there is no imaginable future in which one can imagine an end to celebrity and fame and mass media attention, there is a prospect that the fame-inflation and boundary-blurring that has been happening over the past decade may finally be losing its impetus.

Celebrity Big Brother Experiment

Unlike earlier versions *Celebrity Big Brother* 2006 would take the form of an unprecedented media experiment, an experiment designed to act as a cultural barometer charting who could constitute and, crucially, be accepted as a celebrity within contemporary British society. . . . A failed applicant for *Big Brother 6*, Chantelle Houghton was actually a non-celebrity. She had been selected by the show's producers and set a special task on entering the Big Brother house: to maintain a front in order to convince the rest of her housemates that she too was a celebrity, a pop singer with a girl band who had had one minor UK hit single. If she failed in this project, she would be instantly evicted from the house. But her tenure in the house was sealed when she survived a *Big Brother* task that compelled the housemates to organize themselves in a line in order of their famousness. Out of the lineup of eleven, Chantelle came ninth, and her position in the house was thus secured. Moreover, as Paul Flynn notes: "She pulled off the deception with casual aplomb, warming to her fake ID as a pop star in the imaginary five-strong girl group Kandy Floss ('With a K!')"; and it was Chantelle who would survive the voting process and who would become the eventual *Celebrity Big Brother* winner in a finale that attained a record 7.5 million viewers.

Julie Anne Taddeo and Ken Dvorak, eds.,
The Tube Has Spoken: Reality TV and History.
Lexington: University Press of Kentucky, 2010.

The middle class may continue to sneer at *The X Factor* contestants [who compete as singers], or *Strictly Come Dancing* wannabes, but they are at least people who have tried to do something deftly, or well. The pure nonentity celebrity—

the dedicated D-lister—is, on the other hand, facing a fall in their fortunes. That is to be welcomed if only for the reason that it means that genuinely earned fame will become more apparent and more prominent as the forest of faces and egos thins out, leaving only forms in view that are possessed of reasonable substance.

When that happens, what you might call the liberal panic against celebrity may dissolve and we can start to see fame for what it is—not simply the addiction, like cigarettes, of the simple-minded and/or poor (or "common" as my mother would have called them) but something that has a function for society. That function is to advertise those who do well, and to reward those people and, ultimately, to generate inspiration among those who watch them from a distance.

The ostentatious dance of fame remains distasteful to the aesthete, and I understand why—my self-disgust after watching an episode of CBB is worse even than when I slip out for a crafty quarter pounder with cheese—but a reformed celebrity culture, I would assert, is actually better than no celebrity culture at all. Celebrity culture never could disappear of course. Fame is too resilient and will not endure merely 15 minutes but forever. If it weren't so, we would lose a lot of colour and encouragement from our lives. The key thing is the quality of the fame—and the good news is, over the past six months or so, that quality has been slowly, almost imperceptibly, getting better and better.

> "Figures such as [Susan] Boyle are in-
> voked as culturally reassuring evidence
> of the fact that 'talent'—in itself an
> ideological construct that is never
> clearly defined—still exists."

Celebrity Culture Still Rests on Traditional Myths About Fame

Su Holmes

Su Holmes is Reader in the School of Art, Media, and American Studies at the University of East Anglia. In the following view-point, she argues that fame continues to be linked to traditional ideas about success and to stereotypical gender roles. She points to Susan Boyle, whose rise to stardom through reality television was linked to narratives about ordinary people gaining success through talent. She also discusses the discomfort surrounding the fact that Boyle was middle-aged and not conventionally attrac-tive. Holmes concludes that celebrity is not a democratizing force, since it always depends on a hierarchy of attention and power.

As you read, consider the following questions:

1. According to Holmes, how did Susan Boyle become famous?

2. According to Holmes, how was Boyle's discussion of her background (unemployed and single) greeted by judges on *Britain's Got Talent*?

3. Why does Holmes believe that Boyle attracted so much attention in America, when this is uncommon for British reality TV stars?

Susan Boyle's audition of "I Dreamed a Dream" (*Les Misérables*) on the popular reality format *Britain's Got Talent* (2007–09) rapidly became a phenomenal YouTube hit, catapulting her into media visibility on a global scale. Indeed, viewings of her audition performance leapt from 1.5 million to 5 million in under twenty-four hours. But after being variously hailed as an exceptional talent or a "hairy angel," the speculation surrounding the forty-eight-year-old Scottish church volunteer took on a different tone as media coverage speculated whether she would "triumph or crack" as the eve of the final loomed.

The Success Myth

Debates about the value, "state," and future of modern fame have become increasingly pervasive in academic and popular media contexts, and "ordinary" people have emerged as a fertile site for the circulation of such discourses. Whether seen as emblematic of the "cultural decline" thesis (in which we have witnessed a "regrettable" depreciation in the currency of fame) or as attesting to the emergence of a "populist democracy" (in which fame has become a social process that pivots on an egalitarian rhetoric of "leveling down"), "ordinary" people have been foregrounded as emblematic of "change" in celebrity culture.

Yet despite this emphasis on the "new," it is important to recognize continuity—especially with regard to the mythic or ideological functions of fame. For example, the mediation of the "ordinary" person turned star has historically dramatized the possibilities of the success myth, in which "lucky breaks," hard work, "talent," and "ordinariness" are the central hallmarks of stardom. This is especially true of the reality talent shows such as *Pop Idol*, *The X Factor*, and *Britain's Got Talent*, which (unlike *Big Brother*, for example) continue to peddle more traditional myths of fame. Indeed, figures such as Boyle are invoked as culturally reassuring evidence of the fact that "talent"—in itself an ideological construct that is never clearly defined—still exists (and is waiting to be "discovered") in a context in which "merit" appears to be an absent discourse where celebrity is concerned.

Yet such programs undoubtedly work through more traditional myths of fame within a more self-consciously commercialized modern celebrity culture. In this regard, they are often paradigmatic of a competing war between more traditional myths of fame (in which fame is explained by the existence of an "innate" attribute or talent) and the increasing prevalence—since the post-war period—of manufacture as an explanation for fame (with an emphasis on image construction, packaging, "hype"). Given that the prevalence of manufacture and commerciality offers a potential challenge to more elite (and thus less egalitarian) explanations of fame, particular representational tropes have emerged to paper over the apparent disjunctive here. As Joshua Gamson has explained, one such trope is the increased emphasis on audience agency ("*you* choose"), which appears to insist, "If *you* don't like me, *you* can throw the spotlight onto someone more 'worthy.'"

But in relation to reality TV, the question of audience agency is also invoked with regard to the relationship between "ordinary" people and the ethics of fame. In contrast to the emphasis on a "democratizing" impulse, reality TV has often been yoked to the worst "excesses" of a deeply commercialized celebrity culture in which ordinary people are exploited and used up before being "spat out" by the media machine. Indeed, when it was announced that Boyle was admitted to the Priory clinic after losing to dance troupe Diversity in the final of the show, it was not simply the producers of the program who were invoked as dangerously exposing the singer (who had reportedly also suffered from a mental defect since birth) to the pressures of fame: The viewing public was also seen as colluding in this "irresponsible" act. (After all, hadn't "we" ultimately failed to judge her as the winner?) Either way, the trajectory of Boyle's experience with notoriety reignited debates about the ethics of care provided by reality shows.

Sexism and Celebrity

This framework is particularly resonant with regard to the audition clip that catapulted Boyle into media visibility. As Boyle appears on the audition stage, the choreography of the sequence immediately invites the question, What sort of pleasures will this performance provide? She explains that she is unemployed and single, has "never been kissed," and lives with her cat, Pebbles; she then elaborates on her dream to become a successful singer in the mold of Elaine Page. We then shift between a series of reaction shots in which the panel of judges as well as members of the audience express a combination of disbelief and scorn at what is seen as the apparent disjuncture between Boyle's physical appearance, social status, and professed aspirations. In this regard the sequence offers a somewhat predetermined subject position in which a superior, judging gaze is directed at a seemingly "deluded" subject, her middle-aged status and physical appearance apparently making her desires even more unacceptable than those of the typically young, fame-seeking "wannabe."

In this respect, it is clear that the cultural construction of Boyle intersects with wider gender ideologies that presently structure the meanings of celebrity culture. Both academic and popular attention is now being given to the highly *gendered* imbalance that differentiates the coverage of male and female celebrities, given that current codes for celebrity representation tend to synthesize sexist and ageist logics. Although this is a wider topic that cannot be considered in detail here, it is clear that current celebrity representation is "punishing of young and midlife women in related, but distinctly different, ways." Indeed, it is worth noting that the apparent "disjuncture" between perceived appearance and perceived talent was not cued as so pronounced when Paul Potts, the overweight opera singer who won the first series of *Britain's Got Talent*, auditioned in 2007: judge Simon Cowell noted, "I wasn't expecting that," while fellow panelist Piers Morgan agreed, "You have an incredible voice." Yet the fact that Boyle's performance was seen as so utterly incongruous with her physical appearance was not completely overlooked by journalists writing in the "quality" press. As Tanya Gold observed in the *Guardian*, "Why are we so shocked when 'ugly' women can do things, rather than sitting at home weeping and wishing they were somebody else? Men are allowed to be ugly and talented. Business magnate Alan Sugar looks like a burst bag of flour. Celebrity chef Gordon Ramsay has a dried up riverbed for a face." Yet the initial reaction of the crowd at Boyle's audition suggested that she might "be hanged for her presumption" that she might be worthy of the media spotlight. Furthermore, when Boyle wiggled her hips and explained that her "ordinary" life was "only one side of [her]," judge Piers Morgan winced while the audience tittered with embarrassment, and as Gold later noted: "Didn't Susan know that she wasn't supposed to be sexual?" In observing how Boyle subsequently had her appearance "picked over" in many media forums, it was later observed that "fairy stories are full of woodcutter's daughters who get transformed into princesses, but what's happened to poor Susan Boyle has much more in common with a freakshow."

Always Hierarchical

The promise and expectation of physical transformation referenced in this quote may also elucidate the fervor with which Boyle attracted attention in America (especially when reality TV stars are conventionally national, rather than international, in appeal). Indeed, the expectation that Boyle might dramatize the possibilities of the reflexive self so central to the transformative, consumerist, and individualist ethos of makeover culture appeared to be especially pronounced in her U.S. circulation and reception. To be sure, the fact that constructions of fame are gendered is hardly a startling revelation, but the circulation of Boyle (and the intensity of her media visibility and rapid temporal rise to fame) appears to articulate these in a condensed and thus microcosmic form. Furthermore, while Boyle might initially be invoked as reassuring evidence of the fact that real "talent" still exists (and that it can be discovered by reality shows), she has simultaneously been constructed as the "freakish exception that proves the rule." In this regard, her construction and reception shore up conceptions of acceptable/"unacceptable" norms of femininity (especially as endorsed by celebrity culture), while she is simultaneously hailed as evidence of a democratized fame culture—even though by "raising Susan up, we will forgive ourselves for grinding every other Susan into the dust." As [Graeme] Turner reminds us, fame is a very curious culture site in which to look for evidence of "democratization," given that, no matter how much it appears to expand, celebrity will always be a "hierarchical and exclusive phenomenon, no matter how much it appears to proliferate."

> *"Even hunter-gatherer societies in which material goods are relatively scarce have status hierarchies."*

Celebrity Culture Is Based on Evolution

Stephanie Pappas

Stephanie Pappas is a senior writer for LiveScience. In the following viewpoint, she reports that experts believe celebrity worship is rooted in evolution. Humans are social creatures and naturally look to high-status individuals for guidance in how to behave. Pappas says that in our own culture, interest in celebrity can fill social needs, providing topics of common interest to discuss. She says that in rare cases, fandom can turn into obsession, which can be dangerous to the fan and to others.

As you read, consider the following questions:

1. According to Pappas, from where did the white wedding dress come?

2. What are parasocial relationships, according to the viewpoint?

3. According to Pappas, what personality traits can lead fans to become stalkers?

From the Oscars' red carpet to the tabloids lining super-market checkout lines, celebrity obsession is everywhere. Even the most casual moviegoer might find him or herself flipping through a slide show of Academy Award fashion after the big event. So why do we fixate on celebrities?

In most cases, it's perfectly natural. Humans are social creatures, psychologists say, and we evolved—and still live—in an environment where it paid to pay attention to the people at the top. Celebrity fascination may be an outgrowth of this tendency, nourished by the media and technology.

"In our society, celebrities act like a drug," said James Houran, a psychologist at the consulting firm HVS Executive Search who helped create the first questionnaire to measure celebrity worship. "They're around us everywhere. They're an easy fix."

The Evolution of an Oscar Viewer

It's only relatively recently in human history that people have had near-constant access to celebrity news and gossip. But celebrities themselves are nothing new. People have long looked to monarchs for social, and even fashion, cues: The now ubiquitous white wedding dress caught on after Queen Victoria wore one in 1840.

Even hunter-gatherer societies in which material goods are relatively scarce have status hierarchies, said Daniel Kruger, an evolutionary psychologist at the University of Michigan. Other primate species also keep a close eye on the dominant individuals in their groups.

"There's a few different reasons for that," Kruger told LiveScience. "One is just learning what high-status individuals do so you might more effectively become one, and two, it's basically political. Knowing what is going on with high-status individuals, you'd be better able to navigate the social scene."

Whether [actor] Brad Pitt is on good terms with his ex [actress] Jennifer Aniston isn't likely to affect the average person's life one way or another, of course, but the social tendency to care is deeply ingrained, Kruger said.

Twittering Stars

Stars and the media exploit this tendency. Celebrities give interviews, share juicy information about their personal lives, and even engage directly with fans on sites such as Twitter. The result is that "parasocial" relationships—the psychological term for the kind of one-sided relationships fans have with stars—are easier than ever.

And reaching stardom seems also to be easier than ever. "You have so many opportunities for celebrities to develop, because there are so many platforms," said Stuart Fischoff, an emeritus professor of media psychology at the University of California, Los Angeles. "There's this explosion of celebrity possibility."

Much celebrity obsession is intentionally cultivated, Kruger said. Talk show hosts, for example, try to foster a personal connection with their audience.

"It's savvy marketing," Kruger said.

From Fan to Fanatic

Most of the time, caring about celebrities is no big deal. Even for some obsessed fans, celebrity worship can provide a social outlet they wouldn't have otherwise had, Fischoff told LiveScience. For the seriously shy, celebrity fandom can act as a "psychological prosthesis," he said.

"If they weren't going to be interacting with people otherwise, this makes them at least have a social relationship they didn't have before," Fischoff said. "So it's making the best out of a bad deal, psychologically."

Celebrity Stalking

Although the vast majority of stalking victims are ordinary citizens who know their stalkers, celebrity stalking by rabid fans is increasingly commonplace. The reasons for this recent increase may include various interrelated factors, such as celebrity news television programs, 24-hour cable news networks, the Internet, and the ever present paparazzi. But whatever the cause, stalking is now too often a fact of celebrity life.

Many celebrities, both male and female, have been stalked. One court, in discussing the alleged stalking of *Saturday Night Live* producer Lorne Michaels, listed several other celebrity stalking cases including that of actress Uma Thurman, television host David Letterman, fashion model and television host Tyra Banks, soccer player David Beckham, singers Madonna and Janet Jackson, actress Jodie Foster, and, with tragic consequences, musician John Lennon [who was shot and killed]. Further evidence of the connection between celebrities and stalking is that the first anti-stalking statute was passed in California in 1990, following actress Rebecca Schaeffer's murder by an obsessed fan. Prior to her untimely death in 1989, Schaeffer had starred on the television sitcom *My Sister Sam*.

Tom J. Ferber and Stephen F. Huff,
"New York Law and Procedure," in Entertainment Litigation.
Ed. Charles J. Harder. New York: Oxford University Press, 2011.

There are lines, though. Houran and his colleagues found that it's too simplistic to divide fans into casual, healthy types and wild-eyed stalkers. In fact, celebrity worship is a continuum, Houran told LiveScience.

"The bad news is, there's a stalker in all of us," he said.

When celebrity worship goes overboard, it usually starts out benign, Houran said. People enjoy the escapism of celebrity gossip and bond with others over a favorite star. Next, there's a shift. The person starts thinking of the celebrity constantly, withdrawing from family and friends. Addictive and compulsive behaviors come into play.

Finally, a very few people reach what's known as the "borderline pathological" stage, in which they believe they have a close relationship with their favorite celebrity and take that belief quite seriously. When asked if they'd do something illegal at the request of their favorite celebrity, these people say "yes."

Personality plays a role in pushing people along the path to celebrity stalker-hood, Houran said. People who are egocentric or who have personality traits such as irritability, impulsivity and moodiness are more susceptible. The environment matters, too. People are more susceptible to over-the-top celebrity worship when they're in a phase of identity adjustment. If a person is going through a divorce, loses a job or is having relationship problems, celebrity obsession may be a life raft they cling to.

This identity factor may be why teenagers are so susceptible to worshipping Justin Bieber or their favorite sports star. Younger people, who are still establishing their identities, are more susceptible to celebrity obsession, Houran said.

"Celebrity worship, at its heart, seems to fill something in a person's life," he said. "It gives them a sense of identity, a sense of self. It feeds a psychological need."

> *"Determining whether readers are watching an 'authentic' individual or a performed 'celebrity' persona is not entirely the point; it is the uncertainty that creates pleasure for the celebrity-watcher on Twitter."*

Social Media Does Not Necessarily Create Authentic Connections with Celebrities

Alice Marwick and danah boyd

Alice Marwick is an assistant professor at Fordham University and an academic affiliate at the Center on Law and Information Policy (CLIP) at Fordham University School of Law. danah boyd is a researcher at Microsoft Research; a research assistant professor in the Department of Media, Culture, and Communication at New York University; and a fellow at Harvard's Berkman Center for Internet and Society. In the following viewpoint, the authors argue that celebrities manage their social media presence in order to present the appearance of intimacy. They say that fans are not necessarily experiencing authentic connections with

Alice Marwick and danah boyd, "To See and Be Seen: Celebrity Practice on Twitter," *Convergence*, vol. 17, no. 2, 2011. Copyright © 2011 by Sage Publications, Ltd. All rights reserved. Reproduced by permission.

celebrities; instead, fans are playing a game in which part of the fun is guessing at whether the celebrity interaction is real. The authors argue that interactions with a celebrity on social media are based on maintaining a power differential, in which the celebrity's status is affirmed.

As you read, consider the following questions:

1. According to the viewpoint, what is a "context collapse"?

2. Why do the authors say that we should not judge the closeness of Twitter as false or second best?

3. According to Lionel Trilling, what is the difference between authenticity and sincerity?

Social media technologies let people connect by creating and sharing content. We examine the use of Twitter by famous people to conceptualize celebrity as a practice. On Twitter, celebrity is practiced through the appearance and performance of 'backstage' access. Celebrity practitioners reveal what appears to be personal information to create a sense of intimacy between participant and follower, publicly acknowledge fans, and use language and cultural references to create affiliations with followers. Interactions with other celebrity practitioners and personalities give the impression of candid, uncensored looks at the people behind the personas. But the indeterminate 'authenticity' of these performances appeals to some audiences, who enjoy the game playing intrinsic to gossip consumption. While celebrity practice is theoretically open to all, it is not an equalizer or democratizing discourse. Indeed, in order to successfully practice celebrity, fans must recognize the power differentials intrinsic to the relationship.

Performing Celebrity on Twitter

Like other public genres of social media, Twitter requires celebrity practitioners to negotiate a complicated social environment where fans, famous people, and intermediaries such as

gossip columnists coexist. These multiple audiences compli-
cate self-presentation, since people present identity differently
based on context. Erving Goffman's 1959 work *The Presenta-
tion of Self in Everyday Life* suggested that people, like actors,
navigate 'frontstage' and 'backstage' areas in any given social
situation. This can be understood in terms of place. For instance, a restaurant's floor is frontstage, since employees must
interact in front of an audience of bosses and customers.
More candid talk between servers can take place backstage,
away from the watchful eye of the employer. These concepts
can also be understood in terms of content. For instance, intimate details about one's life are understood as part of the
'backstage' while professional communications can be seen as
a 'frontstage' performance. However, frontstage and backstage
are always relative as they depend on audience, context, and
interpretation.

Goffman's work is related to symbolic interactionism, a
sociological perspective which maintains that meaning is constructed through language, interaction, and interpretation.
Symbolic interactionists claim that identity and self are con-
stituted through constant interactions with others—primarily,
talk. Individuals work together to uphold preferred self-images
of themselves and their conversation partners, through strategies like maintaining (or 'saving') face, collectively encouraging social norms, or negotiating power differentials and dis-
agreements. What Goffman refers to as 'impression
management' takes place through ongoing adjustment to perceptions of audience judgment.

Very famous people constantly navigate complex identity
performances. The ostensible disconnect between a famous
person's public persona and 'authentic' self is fueled by tabloid
magazines, paparazzi photos, and gossip columns that purport
to reveal what a particular starlet is 'really' like. Celebrity scan-
dals often involve the exposure of personal information to the
public, such as outing someone as queer or the dissemination

of photos, 'sex tapes', answering machine messages, emails, and other purportedly backstage documents. This tricky territory has traditionally been navigated with the help of assistants, agents, public relations personnel, bodyguards, and other mechanisms that broker access between famous person and fan. On Twitter, however, this infrastructure is not available. As we will see, celebrity practice involves the appearance and performance of backstage access to the famous, presuming that the typical celebrity persona involves artifice. In Joshua Gamson's taxonomy of celebrity watchers, he writes:

> A good chunk of the audience reads the celebrity text in its own language, recognizing and often playing with the blurriness of its vocabulary. They leave open the questions of authenticity and along with it the question of merit. For them, celebrity is not a prestige system, or a postmodern hall of mirrors, but . . . a game.

Determining whether readers are watching an 'authentic' individual or a performed 'celebrity' persona is not entirely the point; it is the uncertainty that creates pleasure for the celebrity-watcher on Twitter.

Simultaneously, celebrity practice reinforces unequal power differentials. While Twitter users who do not use the site instrumentally may think of their followers as friends or family, celebrity practice necessitates viewing followers as *fans*. Performing celebrity requires that this asymmetrical status is recognized by others. Fans show deference, creating mutual recognition of the status imbalance between practitioner and fan. In return, fan-practitioner relationships move beyond parasocial interaction, the illusion of a 'real', face-to-face friendship with a performer created through watching television shows or listening to music. In parasocial relationships, or what John Thompson calls 'mediated quasi-interaction', a fan responds to a media figure 'as if s/he was a personal acquaintance'; in contrast, Twitter suggests the possibility of interaction. There is no singular formula for celebrity practice; it consists of a set of learned techniques that are leveraged differently by individuals.

Public Recognition and Fan Maintenance

Like much social media, Twitter creates a 'context collapse' in which multiple audiences, usually thought of as separate, co-exist in a single social context. The practice of celebrity involves negotiating these multiple audiences to successfully maintain face and manage impressions. Celebrity practitioners use public acknowledgment, in the form of @replies, to connect with others. Fans @reply to famous people not only in the hope of receiving a reply, but to display a relationship, whether positive or negative. If fans receive @replies back, they function as a mark of status and are publicized within the fan community. Celebrity practitioners' public acknowledgement of friends, peers, and colleagues is rarely critical, primarily adhering to frontstage norms of public appearance. Famous people mention fans to perform connection and availability, give back to loyal followers, and manage their popularity.

Celebrity practice requires constant interaction with fans to preserve the power differentials intrinsic to the performed 'celebrity' and 'fan' personas. Celebrity practitioners approach this in different ways. For example, Soleil Moon Frye, better known as 1980s child actress 'Punky Brewster', frequently tweets inspirational and funny anecdotes about parenting:

> Moonfrye: RT @bklyndafna @Moonfrye DAILY QUOTE
> The future belongs to those who believe in the beauty of their dreams.—Eleanor Roosevelt

Today, Frye runs a children's boutique in LA; her followers are primarily women with children. In this example, bklyndafna tweets an Eleanor Roosevelt quote to Moonfrye in a gesture that resembles gift-giving. This marks bklyndafna as a fan and affiliates her with Moonfrye's general values. To show appreciation, Moonfrye publicly retweets (RT) the quote to her followers, retaining bklyndafna's original attribution. This mutual public recognition of commonality allows Moonfrye to articulate ongoing connections with her followers.

People spending time with other Twitter users online or in person often mention it in their tweets, identifying the other person through the @username convention. For example, when Mariah Carey tweets about her friend Jasmine Dotiwala, an MTV producer and gossip columnist, she chooses to identify her by her Twitter username:

> MariahCarey: @jasminedotiwala just sang the Vegas remix of "these are a few of my favorite things and did a little dance in a terry cloth robe" hilarious

This establishes intimacy between Carey and her followers by sharing personal details from her life while publicly identifying jasminedotiwala as a friend—a performance of backstage access—and inviting her followers to check out Jasmine's Twitter stream. This maintains the power differential between an average fan and the singer's intimate friend, since Jasmine is marked as someone who spends time with Mariah in person. It also provides a public endorsement of Jasmine's Twitter stream. While some highly followed users reference others without being prompted, others will acknowledge friends as a favor to direct attention their way. This is particularly visible through the practice of retweeting:

> KevinRose: RT: @garyvee announcing my 1st business book http://tinyurl.com/garyveebook—congrats to @garyvee, crush it!

> Greggrundberg: RT @WilfridDierkes "watch My Name is Earl tonite cause if it gets canceled my family is moving in w/you." Peeps please watch. Save us all!!

Both these tweets demonstrate publicly articulated relational ties: between Digg founder Kevin Rose and motivational speaker Gary Vaynerchuk, and between actor Greg Grunberg and producer Greg Garcia. This practice suggests insiderness between the participants, but it also highlights the dynamics of attention on Twitter.

Public acknowledgment, of either friends or fans, is not always positive. Twitter user Leproff sends an angry tweet to Republican politician Newt Gingrich about [former US president Ronald] Reagan, who responds tersely:

> Leproff: @newtgingrich I do not agree when you say that USSR collapsed because of Ronald Reagan. This is a historical lie!

> NewtGingrich: @Leproff do you really believe the soviet union would have disappeared without reagab. Read peter schweizers book reagans war

Gingrich's tweet reinforces his image as an ornery conservative, but the act of responding also shows that he takes time to talk directly with followers. The potential of such interactions implies that fans are faced with accountability to the actors and singers they gossip about. Some famous people directly address gossip, for instance:

> LilyRoseAllen: and no i didnt say that stuff, ive never met cheryl, or her husband, noe david beckham. please dont believe that rubbish.

> NewtGingrich: A false story was planted this morning about my sueing twitter. This is totally false and we have repudiated it with the media

> Hollymadison123: @PerezHilton Criss and i r not back together.. lol!

Rumor-mongering, whether by follower or gossip columnist Perez Hilton, can theoretically be directly corrected. Of course, fans may choose to believe the rumor even if the famous person chooses to reject it and not all fans read all tweets written by a celebrity. As with any other medium, correcting a rumor on Twitter can be more challenging than starting one.

While gossiping about celebrities is a common practice that creates social bonds and provides a frame for discussion of larger issues, participants on Twitter run the risk of being publicly shamed by the individual they are discussing:

> Trent_Reznor: Perfect example of the kind of complete parasitic delusional asshole that makes you regret fame: @AngieZherself.

> Trent_Reznor: And you're not anonymous dear, you are Angela L. Zajac from Worcester with a criminal record.

While Trent Reznor's decision to publicly shame one of his fans may be seen as an attempt to gain control and push back against someone that he perceives as an 'asshole', this too may backfire. There are plenty who seek attention and will settle for negative attention. While public relations professionals and magazine editors traditionally managed information flow through spin control or strategic censorship, Twitter gossip may be silenced through direct acknowledgment from celebrity practitioners. At the same time, it may also be ignited.

Affiliation

Affiliation is the process of publicly performing a connection between practitioners and fans using language, words, cultural symbols, and conventions. Teen rapper Soulja Boy's use of language is virtually identical to that of his audience, primarily young hip-hop fans ('That song me & Lola did is Bumpin in the whip my speakers goin ham!'). P. Diddy uses inspirational and inclusive language to ally himself with his followers: 'Let's stay focused to day people! Today can be the start of a positive change in our lives. Claim it and do it!!!! Just do

Top Ten Most Followed on Twitter, August 2014			
Twitter user	Followers	Following	Tweets
Katy Perry	55,948,380	155	6,029
Justin Bieber	53,911,126	141,034	27,558
Barack Obama	45,538,888	648,580	12,308
YouTube	44,584,414	716	11,083
Taylor Swift	42,944,947	134	2,336
Lady Gaga	41,958,406	134,088	5,233
Britney Spears	38,560,745	402,114	3,732
Rihanna	36,890,048	1,141	9,284
Instagram	34,611,229	17	5,324
Justin Timberlake	34,096,266	81	2,484

TAKEN FROM: TwitterCounter, "Twitter Top 100 Most Followers," August 25, 2014.

it!!!' Soleil Moon Frye tells stories about the difficulties of child-rearing that emphasize the similarities between herself and her primarily female followers. Mariah Carey's fans have a language ('HBF', 'lambs', 'LYM') that create linguistic ties with each other and their favorite singer.

Links and retweets provide good examples of the affiliative use of cultural markers and symbols. Generally, highly followed users RT or link to items that interest them and presumably their followers. In these examples, liberal pundit Rachel Maddow and actor Ashton Kutcher send out URLs:

Maddow: Remember that wicked scary job loss chart? Here it is among budget docs with some of its wicked scary chart friends (pdf!) http://is.gd/l1AJ

@aplusk: this is amazing thanks 4 sharing RT @ShaynaSkim: A guy single-handedly starts a dance party! MUST WATCH http://bit.ly/wh4cA

Maddow links to a White House–provided PDF of economic charts, implying that her followers—news junkies, policy wonks, and armchair economists—would find it interesting. Maddow is not tweeting about her life, but a common interest she shares with her followers. In contrast, Ashton Kutcher RTs a funny video of a concert-goer dancing to indie artist Santigold. (Note that both are using URL shortening services, which abbreviate long web addresses to fit Twitter's 140 character limit.) The cultural markers in this tweet—hip music, an outdoor music festival, goofy dancing—affiliate Kutcher with his teen and 20-something base. These links are presumably chosen both to provide value to their fan base and to emphasize commonalities between the practitioner and his or her followers.

Intimacy

Twitter allows celebrity practitioners to create a sense of closeness and familiarity between themselves and their followers. Highly followed accounts vary in performed intimacy; while some mostly broadcast information about an upcoming tour or book, others write about personal subjects, post exclusive content, or chat about their daily lives. This type of strategic revealing found on confessional talk show appearances, tell-all autobiographies, and magazine interviews has been criticized as 'second order intimacy' or the 'illusion of intimacy'. This point of view maintains that performed intimacy is synonymous with parasocial interaction and a poor substitute for actual interaction.

While it is true that the practice of celebrity involves strategically managed self-disclosure, we should not be so quick to judge the closeness created by Twitter as false and second-best. First, Twitter does provide the possibility of actual interaction with the highly followed person, in the form of a direct message or @reply. Second, the 'lifestreaming' function of Twitter encourages 'digital intimacy'. The many seemingly insignificant messages serve as phatic communication; rather than sharing meaningful information, many tweets serve a social function, reinforcing connections and maintaining social bonds. If we accept that Twitter creates a sense of ongoing connection with one's real-life acquaintances and friends, following a famous person's tweets over a period of time may create an equally valid feeling of 'knowing' them. Finally, as we will see in the following case studies, users can and do let things slip via Twitter that would never be revealed in an interview with *People* magazine.

On Twitter, performative intimacy is practiced by posting personal pictures and videos, addressing rumors, and sharing personal information. Picture-hosting services, such as YFrog and Twitpic, allow users directly to post camera phone pictures to Twitter. Famous people frequently use these services, creating the illusion of first-person glimpses into their lives. Ashton Kutcher, for example, tweets pictures of himself on set, during talk show appearances, and posing with his wife Demi Moore and celebrities such as actress Mischa Barton and R&B singer Usher. Pop singer Katy Perry posts pictures of her nails, her tour bus, and her meals while performing around the world. Similarly, streaming video services like Ustream are used by musicians like Bow Wow and Snoop Dogg to broadcast studio recordings and live performances, while others post funny videos, take questions from fans, or host live events. Shaquille O'Neal, for instance, filmed himself lip-synching and tweeted the link to his followers. While these pictures and videos add a visual dimension, they are still strategically chosen by the practitioner, in contrast to the unauthorized candids found in tabloids and gossip blogs.

As we have seen, other famous people use Twitter to directly address rumors. The same technique is used to respond to fan criticism or comments. For instance, Shaq retorted to a follower who said his sneakers were ugly:

> @Naimthestar yea dats why I sold 80 million pair since 1992
> at 3 dollars per pair comn to me, do the math

In addition to publicly recognizing and responding to a fan concern, this information makes the fan feel that they possess insider, candid knowledge about the sports star. Contentious discussions are not uncommon:

Jake_Banks: @ddlovato the Jonas Brothers, are just a disney fabrication who did not earn their fame and thusly are undeserving of such a large spotlight

Ddlovato: @Jake_Banks It's funny that you call them a "disney fabrication" but they have fans of ALL ages and they do deserve the spotlight.

Ddlovato: They've been touring and working extremely hard for years and they still haven't stopped. They're the hardest working people I know of.

Lacey22211: @lilyroseallen why dont u just accept anyone on ur myspace? its a f------ music page! wtf??? C---

LilyRoseAllen: @lacey22211 because people spam my page, and post loads of noise as comments.

These exchanges demonstrate how Twitter has contributed to changes in the parasocial dynamic. While parasocial interaction is largely imaginary and takes place primarily in the fan's mind, Twitter conversations between fans and famous people are public and visible, and involve direct engagement between the famous person and their follower. The fan's ability to engage in discussion with a famous person depathologizes the parasocial and recontextualizes it within a medium that the follower may use to talk to real-life acquaintances. As we have seen, Twitter makes fans accountable for rude comments, taking the subjects of gossip out of the realm of fantasy and repositioning them as 'real people'. Traditional settings for in-person celebrity-fan interactions, such as autograph signings and award ceremonies, are highly managed and limited in scope. In contrast, although Twitter conversations are mediated, they appear off-the-cuff, contributing to a sense that the reader is seeing the real, authentic person behind the 'celebrity'.

Authenticity and Sincerity

In *Sincerity and Authenticity*, Lionel Trilling distinguishes authenticity from sincerity. He conceptualizes authenticity as a display of the hidden inner life, complete with passions and anguish, while sincerity is the opposite of hypocrisy—honesty without pretense. Both these elements matter on Twitter. The intimacy engendered by celebrity tweets provide the glimpse into the inner life that fans want, while at the most basic level, fans want to ensure that the person tweeting is sincerely who they claim to be. Twitter is generally a site where personal disclosure and intimacy are normative, so access, intimacy, and affiliation are valueless if an account is fake or written by an assistant. The process involved in vetting whether a person is really who they claim to be reveals the appeal of celebrity practice for fans: the potential for disclosing the 'truth', the uncensored person stripped of PR artifice and management.

Users frequently debate whether Twitter accounts are written by who they claim to be. The site truthtweet.com verifies or debunks accounts like Tina_Fey and The_Pitts. During our research, accounts for Seth Rogen, Michael Phelps, and Tina Fey were identified as impostors and subsequently shut down (Tina_Fey was renamed 'FakeTinaFey' and the comedian Tina Fey took over Tina_Fey). Some of these demonstrably false accounts are valued for their satirical value or effective impersonation, such [as] 'FakeSarahPalin' [satirizing the conservative 2008 vice-presidential candidate] whose tweets include things like 'This "death panel" thing is really taking off! Suck it, Luntz, you got p0wned Palin style. Srsly!!!' In June 2009, Twitter introduced verified accounts that certify 'genuine' famous people. As previously discussed, not all 'celebrity' accounts are written by the purported individual. In our own efforts to account for authenticity of Twitter accounts, we focused on the *signals* of authenticity. Judith Donath discusses how subtle online signals function as identity cues, given the dearth of physical evidence. Given the presence of typos in most participants' tweets, we expect that 'real' celebrity practitioners will make grammatical or spelling mistakes. Tweets that are personal, controversial, or negative—in other words, that contradict the stereotype of the overly managed 'celebrity' account—signal greater authenticity than safely vetted publicity messages. If the writer interacted with fans, used the first-person voice, and posted candid snapshots, they seemed more authentic, as did their use of mobile clients such as Tweetie or TwitterBerry. Of course, our assessment is only based on the available signals; we have no way of validating our best guesses. Similarly, fans carefully evaluate the *sincerity* of celebrity accounts.

Trilling's alternative meaning of authenticity, as passion and interiority, is also crucial to Twitter's appeal. 'Authenticity' is a social construct that is ultimately always relative and context dependent; it seems that self-disclosure, and therefore what it *means* to be authentic, is expected more on Twitter compared to other venues. While we accept that a *Cosmopolitan* cover story on pop star Katy Perry will probably be a bit boring, we anticipate that Perry's Twitter feed will be in keeping with her glamorous, wacky image. Celebrity practice that sticks to the safe and publicly consumable risks being viewed as inauthentic, while successful celebrity practice suggests intimacy, disclosure, and connection.

Periodical and Internet Sources Bibliography

The following articles have been selected to supplement the diverse views presented in this chapter.

Philip Cohen	"How Celebrities Use Social Media to Build Their Brand," *Social Media Today,* June 24, 2013.
Joe Coscarelli	"Who Did You Think Teenagers Were Watching on Their Phones?," *New York,* April 20, 2014.
Thomas Clayton	"5 Ways Celebrities' Social Media Presence Evolved in 2012," *Huffington Post,* January 22, 2013.
Grace Duffy	"Column: Celebrity Culture Is Becoming Toxic and Leading Us to Set Impossible Standards," *TheJournal.ie* (Ireland), March 16, 2013.
Megan Gannon	"Obit Archives Reveal Rise of Celebrity Culture," LiveScience, August 14, 2012.
Kate Knibbs	"How Social Media Has Changed What It Means to Be a Celebrity," Digital Trends, April 15, 2013.
Haydn Shaughnessy	"When Social Media Met Celebrity (and Fell in Love, Authentically)," *Forbes,* February 19, 2012.
Lydia Snapper	"Celebrity Culture and YouTube," Streamline Buzzer, May 15, 2014.
Marlow Stern	"Sofia Coppola on 'The Bling Ring,' Celebrity Culture, Kanye West, More," *Daily Beast,* June 13, 2013.
Tiffany Vega	"Twitter: A Way to Network and Feel Closer to Celebrities," *Salem State Log* (Massachusetts), February 16, 2012.

For Further Discussion

Chapter 1

1. After reading the viewpoints in this chapter, do you think celebrity culture is harmful? If so, what do you feel is the most harmful aspect? If not, what are some of the positive aspects of celebrity culture? Use evidence from the viewpoints to support your answer.

2. Landon Y. Jones contends that people are more interested in celebrities than real-life heroes. Do you agree or disagree with Jones, and why?

3. Tara Haelle argues that celebrity athletes endorse unhealthy food and drinks, and these endorsements target teens. Why does Haelle think such endorsements are harmful? Do you agree with Haelle's argument? Why, or why not?

Chapter 2

1. Based on the viewpoints in this chapter, do you think celebrity activism is beneficial? Why, or why not? Present examples from the viewpoints to defend your answer.

2. Alain de Botton maintains that admiring celebrities who engage in good causes can be helpful. What are the author's main reasons for making this claim? Do you agree or disagree with the author, and why?

3. Anderson Antunes reports on the most generous celebrities and how their donations benefit charities. Conversely, Kat Stoeffel contends that celebrity philanthropy has risks. After reading the viewpoints, explain why you think celebrity philanthropy is either harmful or beneficial. Use evidence from the viewpoints to support your answer.

Chapter 3

1. After reading the viewpoints in this chapter, what group mentioned do you think is most affected by celebrity culture? Is this group affected in a positive or negative way? Cite evidence from the viewpoints to support your answer.

2. Jeremy W. Peters argues that when celebrities come out as lesbian, gay, or bisexual it does not generate as much publicity as the announcement would have made in the past, except when the individual making the announcement is from a conservative community. Why does Peters think this makes a difference? Do you agree with Peters's assessment of celebrity announcements regarding their sexuality? Explain your reasoning.

3. Meghan Murphy argues that celebrities are not experts on feminism and often know little about the topic; therefore, asking a celebrity if she is a feminist only contributes to the confusion surrounding what feminism actually is. Cite examples from Murphy's viewpoint that demonstrate this argument. Why do you think reporters continually ask female celebrities if they are feminists? Explain your reasoning.

Chapter 4

1. How is celebrity culture changing? Explain some of the factors that are shaping celebrity culture in the twenty-first century. Use evidence from the viewpoints to support your reasoning.

2. Stephanie Pappas asserts that celebrity worship is based on evolution. Why does the author believe this is true? Do you agree with this argument? Why, or why not?

3. Alice Marwick and danah boyd maintain that on Twitter, fans do not necessarily experience genuine connections with celebrities. What evidence do the authors provide to

support this argument? Do you agree with Marwick and boyd? Cite text from the viewpoint to support your answer.

Organizations to Contact

The editors have compiled the following list of organizations concerned with the issues debated in this book. The descriptions are derived from materials provided by the organizations. All have publications or information available for interested readers. The list was compiled on the date of publication of the present volume; the information provided here may change. Be aware that many organizations take several weeks or longer to respond to inquiries, so allow as much time as possible.

Academy of Motion Picture Arts and Sciences

8949 Wilshire Boulevard, Beverly Hills, California   90211
(310) 247-3000 • fax: (310) 859-9619
website: www.oscars.org

Founded in 1927, the Academy of Motion Picture Arts and Sciences is an honorary membership organization that includes more than six thousand artists and professionals who work in the film industry, including actors, directors, producers, designers, writers, and cinematographers. The academy is dedicated to the advancement of the arts and sciences of motion pictures. Each year, it presents the Academy Awards, also known as the Oscars. The academy's Media Literacy Program is designed to help students become aware of media messages encountered daily, improve analytical skills to evaluate those messages, and encourage provocative and thoughtful interaction with the media.

American Psychological Association (APA)

750 First Street NE, Washington, DC   20002-4242
(800) 374-2721
website: www.apa.org

The American Psychological Association (APA) is a scientific and professional organization that represents psychologists in the United States and Canada. With more than 135,000 members, the APA is the largest association of psychologists worldwide. It publishes articles and reports related to popular culture, celebrities, children and the media, and similar topics in its numerous magazines and journals, including articles such as "Fame, Facebook, and Twitter: How Attitudes About Fame Predict Frequency and Nature of Social Media Use."

Center for Media and Public Affairs (CMPA)

933 N. Kenmore Street, Suite 405, Arlington, VA 22201

(571) 319-0029 • fax: (571) 319-0034

e-mail: mail@cmpa.com

website: www.cmpa.com

Founded in 1985, the Center for Media and Public Affairs (CMPA) is a nonpartisan research and educational organization that conducts scientific studies of news and entertainment media. It studies the media treatment of social and political affairs and uses surveys to measure the media's influence on public opinion. CMPA's website offers links to many articles, including "Comics Look to Obama, Democrats for Humor" and "The Changed Politics of Late-Night TV."

Center for Media Literacy (CML)

22837 Pacific Coast Highway, #472, Malibu, CA 90265

(310) 804-3985

e-mail: cml@medialit.org

website: www.medialit.org

The Center for Media Literacy (CML) is an educational organization that offers critical analysis of the media through its publications and advocacy. CML works to promote and support media literacy, believing it is an essential skill in the twenty-first century. CML believes individuals should be empowered from a young age to make informed choices about the media they consume. CONNECT!ONS is the official newsletter of the organization, and it features articles such as "Theme: Media and Body Image."

Institute for Advanced Studies in Culture (IASC)
Watson Manor, 3 University Circle, Charlottesville, VA   22903
(434) 924-7705 • fax: (434) 243-5590
e-mail: iasc@virginia.edu
website: www.iasc-culture.org

The Institute for Advanced Studies in Culture (IASC) is a research center and intellectual community at the University of Virginia that studies cultural changes. IASC seeks to understand cultural change and its consequences, trains young scholars, and provides intellectual leadership. Among its publications are articles, survey reports, and the journal the *Hedgehog Review*. IASC's website offers information on its various programs, including the Program on Culture and Formation, which studies how cultural influences, such as celebrity and media, shape the way children are socialized and develop self-identities.

Media Watch
PO Box 618, Santa Cruz, CA   95061
(831) 423-6355
e-mail: info@mediawatch.com
website: www.mediawatch.com

Media Watch is a nonprofit organization that works to challenge stereotypes and biased information in the media through education and action. It also endorses media literacy as part of the educational system. In addition to publishing the monthly *Action Alert* newsletter, Media Watch also posts articles on its website, including "We're Raising Girls Who Hate Their Bodies" and "Privacy Is a Right—Regardless of Who You Are."

ONE
1400 Eye Street, Suite 600, Washington, DC   20005
(202) 495-2700
website: www.one.org/us

Cofounded by Bono, the lead singer of U2, ONE is a coalition made up of nearly six million members and various nonprofit, advocacy, and humanitarian organizations. ONE is a combined effort of two related nonprofit, nonpartisan organizations—the ONE Campaign and ONE Action. ONE's objective is to raise public awareness of global poverty and its effects worldwide. ONE's website contains a wealth of information about its members' humanitarian efforts. In addition, its website offers a blog, press releases, reports, and articles such as "Bono Named Most Politically Effective Celeb of All Time" and "Colin Firth: Why Do You Have to Hear from an Actor?"

Pew Research Center

1615 L Street NW, Suite 700, Washington, DC 20036
(202) 419-4300 • fax: (202) 419-4349
website: www.pewresearch.org

The Pew Research Center is a "fact tank" that provides information on the issues, attitudes, and trends shaping America and the world. It conducts public opinion polls and social science research; reports and analyzes news; and holds forums and briefings. The center's website provides articles and survey reports, including "Celebrity Chasing Online" and "Millennials, Media, and Information."

Popular Culture Association/American Culture Association (PCA/ACA)

website: pcaaca.org

The Popular Culture Association/American Culture Association (PCA/ACA) is a group of scholars and enthusiasts who study popular culture. The PCA/ACA supports the study of popular and American culture and established an endowment fund in 1997 to solidify its commitment to the long-term study of popular culture in all its forms. The PCA/ACA Endowment has been able to support graduate students, international scholars, and researchers interested in popular and American culture studies. PCA/ACA publishes the *Journal of Popular Culture*, which features articles such as "Editorial: The New Television Anti-Hero."

Rutherford Institute
PO Box 7482, Charlottesville, VA   22906-7482
(434) 978-3888 • fax: (434) 978-1789
e-mail: staff@rutherford.org
website: www.rutherford.org

Since its inception in 1982, the Rutherford Institute has been one of the nation's leading advocates of civil liberties and human rights. The organization litigates in the courts and educates the public on a wide range of issues affecting individual freedom in the United States and around the world. It analyzes and reports on celebrity culture in its articles, which include "50 Years After the Beatles: Isn't It Time for Another Political & Cultural Revolution?" and "Miley Cyrus and the Pornification of America."

Screen Actors Guild–American Federation of Television and Radio Artists (SAG-AFTRA)
5757 Wilshire Boulevard, 7th Floor
Los Angeles, CA   90036-3600
(323) 954-1600
e-mail: sagaftrainfo@sagaftra.org
website: www.sagaftra.org

The Screen Actors Guild–American Federation of Television and Radio Artists (SAG-AFTRA) strives to enhance actors' working conditions and compensation and benefits, as well as advocates for artists' rights. SAG-AFTRA represents more than 165,000 actors, recording artists, and others who work in the entertainment industry and the media. SAG-AFTRA publishes a quarterly magazine, which includes articles such as "Making Their Voices Heard."

Bibliography of Books

Robin D. Barnes — *Outrageous Invasions: Celebrities' Private Lives, Media, and the Law.* New York: Oxford University Press, 2010.

Matthew Bishop and Michael Green — *Philanthrocapitalism: How Giving Can Save the World.* New York: Bloomsbury Press, 2009.

Trevor J. Blank — *The Last Laugh: Folk Humor, Celebrity Culture, and Mass-Mediated Disasters in the Digital Age.* Madison, WI: University of Wisconsin Press, 2013.

Dan Brockington — *Celebrity Advocacy and International Development.* New York: Routledge, 2014.

Dan Brockington — *Celebrity and the Environment: Fame, Wealth, and Power in Conservation.* New York: Zed Books, 2009.

Ellis Cashmore — *Celebrity Culture.* New York: Routledge, 2014.

Elizabeth Currid-Halkett — *Starstruck: The Business of Celebrity.* New York: Faber and Faber, 2010.

Amber L. Davisson — *Lady Gaga and the Remaking of Celebrity Culture.* Jefferson, NC: McFarland & Company, 2013.

Kerry O. Ferris and Scott R. Harris — *Stargazing: Celebrity, Fame, and Social Interaction.* New York: Routledge, 2011.

Emily Fox-Kales — *Body Shots: Hollywood and the Culture of Eating Disorders.* Albany: State University of New York Press, 2011.

Gavin Fridell and Martijn Konings, eds. — *Age of Icons: Exploring Philanthrocapitalism in the Contemporary World.* Toronto, ON: University of Toronto Press, 2013.

Adria Y. Goldman, VaNatta S. Ford, Alexa A. Harris, and Natasha R. Howard, eds. — *Black Women and Popular Culture: The Conversation Continues.* Lanham, MD: Lexington Books, 2014.

Barrie Gunter — *Celebrity Capital: Assessing the Value of Fame.* New York: Bloomsbury Academic, 2014.

Marjorie Hallenbeck-Huber — *Celebrities' Most Wanted: The Top 10 Book of Lavish Lifestyles, Tabloid Tidbits, and Other Superstar Oddities.* Washington, DC: Potomac Books, 2010.

Su Holmes and Diane Negra, eds. — *In the Limelight and Under the Microscope: Forms and Functions of Female Celebrity.* New York: Continuum International Publishing Group, 2011.

Sarah J. Jackson — *Black Celebrity, Racial Politics, and the Press: Framing Dissent.* New York: Routledge, 2014.

Ilan Kapoor   *Celebrity Humanitarianism: The
                   Ideology of Global Charity.* New York:
                   Routledge, 2012.

Alice E. Marwick   *Status Update: Celebrity, Publicity,
                   and Branding in the Social Media Age.*
                   New Haven, CT: Yale University
                   Press, 2013.

Erin A. Meyers   *Dishing Dirt in the Digital Age:
                   Celebrity Gossip Blogs and
                   Participatory Media Culture.* New
                   York: Peter Lang Publishing, 2013.

Sarah Projansky   *Spectacular Girls: Media Fascination
                   and Celebrity Culture.* New York: New
                   York University Press, 2014.

Karen   *Celebrity Culture and the American
Sternheimer   Dream: Stardom and Social Mobility.*
                   New York: Routledge, 2011.

Alison Stokes, ed. *It's OK to Be Gay: Celebrity Coming
                   Out Stories.* Abercynon, UK: Accent
                   Press, 2013.

Mark Wheeler   *Celebrity Politics.* Malden, MA: Polity
                   Press, 2013.

Index

A

Academy Awards, 30, 31, 36, 160
Activism, celebrities
  breast-feeding, 62–63
  coming out, 102, 103–105, 106–107, 109–114
  as fashionable, 28, 36, 67–68
  philanthropy and giving, 74–82
  sexual assault prevention, 42–48
  worthy causes receive attention, 64–68
  worthy causes trivialized, 69–73
Addictive behavior, 163
Adele, 129
Adichie Chimamanda Ngozi, 117
Admiration, 65–66, 68
  celebrity role models and emulation, 56, 139, 140
  hero figures, 33, 35
Adoption, 66
Advertising
  endorsements, changing nature, 132–133
  endorsements, charities, 74, 76–77
  endorsements, junk food, 53–59
  grassroots marketing, 140
  viewing critically, 57, 59
  youth surveys, 56–57
AFESIP Cambodia, 85, 86
Affiliation, 171–172
Africa, 64, 67, 89
Ageism, 153, 154, 157

Agreement on Trade-Related Aspects of Intellectual Property Rights (TRIPS; 1994), 93
Allen, Lily, 170, 175
Allende, Isabel, 80
Alpert, Herb, 75, 78
Altruism, motivation, 67–68
  See also Philanthropy and giving
American Paralysis Association, 77
Anonymity assumptions and errors, 171
Anthony, Carmelo, 81
Antunes, Anderson, 74–82
Approval of others, as motivation, 24
Armitage, Simon, 150
Armstrong, Lance, 34, 77, 81
Artists, 150
Athletes
  coming out, 105
  food and drink advertising, 53–59
  philanthropy, 77–82
  Twitter use, 174–175
Audience agency, 155–156
Augustine of Hippo, 23
Authenticity. *See* Honesty and authenticity
Autographs, 143, 144

B

Bailey, Reg, 128–129
Bakhtin, Mikhail, 136, 137, 138
Baldwin, Alec, 80
Banks, Jake, 175
Banks, Tyra, 162

McCoy, David, 91, 95, 96
McGee, Michelle, 39
Media and promotion
blame for celebrity fixation, 21–22
framing and commentary, celebrity incidents, 100–101, 157
magazine covers, 32–33, 35
media power, 135, 137–138, 139, 141–142, 153, 166–167, 170–171
nature as intrusive, 31–32, 100
projects about celebrity itself, 23
traditional vs. newer media, 14, 29, 135, 143, 174, 177
Medieval Europe, 136
Meehan, Patrick, 48
Mental health
celebrity narcissism, 24, 26
celebrity worshippers, 21, 24–25
media judgments, 156
Meyers, Seth, 45
Michaels, Lorne, 162
"Micro-celebrities," 14–16
Microsoft, 89, 93
Milano, Alyssa, 132
Millman, Robert B., 24
Milton, John, 23, 36
Models, 16, 75, 150, 162
Montaigne, Michel de, 23
Moore, Demi, 33, 174
Moral panic, 125, 126, 127, 128–129
Morgan, Piers, 157
Mothers' Union (UK), 128–129
Movie stars
burdens/benefits of celebrity, 23–24
hero portrayals, 30

magazine coverage, 31–36
philanthropy, 78–79
See also specific actors
MTV Video Music Awards, 49, 50–52
Murdered celebrities, 162
Murphy, Meghan, 120–124
Music videos, 125, 126, 128–129
Myths about fame, 153–158

N

National Coming Out Day, 103
New media vs. traditional media, 14, 29, 135, 143, 174, 177
The *New York Times*, 85–87, 102, 110–111, 112
Newlyweds: The First Year (television program), 19
Newman, Paul, 33
Newsweek (periodical), 85, 87, 107
Nigri, Jessica, 15
Nixon, Richard, 31–32
Nolte, Nick, 33
NotAlone.gov, 43, 44, 47

O

Obama, Barack
administration programs against sexual assault, 43, 44–46
Twitter followers, 172
Obama, Michelle, 54
Obsessed fans, 159, 161–163
Omidyar, Pierre, 72
O'Neal, Shaquille, 174–175
Ordinary people
celebrities, humanizing, 175–176
expectations of fame, 21, 41
fame myths, 154–155